"This book was invaluable for a beginning homeschooler like me. What an incredible resource for planning our future as a homeschool family!"–**Heidi Rohland,** *future homeschooler of two*

"I found myself wanting to take a dip into this fun and creative world that Alicia describes throughout the book. I even had moments wishing that I was one of her kids in this home that doesn't live confined to a calendar or clock, but strives to make life the library of learning. Reading this felt like an afternoon of coffee with a close friend that you don't want to end." —**Caryn Jenkins,** *mom of two*

"Homeschooling   's refreshingly simple approach to tackli   izauon an   -two keys to a successful learning environment. Whether re ers are new to homeschooling, or have years of experience, this book gives invaluable tips in how to organize your homeschool while maintaining enough flexibility for everyday life." —**Eryn Bollish,** *homeschooling mom of four*

"*Plan To Be Flexible* is replete with first-hand, Christ-directed examples from her family's school days. Alicia's approach explores how to maintain the utmost confidence as academics, life skills, and spiritual character are instilled—no matter the season of life. I *loved* this book!" —**Kelli Tague,** *veteran homeschooling mom of six*

PLAN TO BE

Designing A Homeschool Year
And Daily Schedule That Works For Your Family

By Alicia Kazsuk

ISBN-13: 978-1490959535
ISBN-10: 149095953X

Acknowledgements

To my friends and writing mentors who took the time to examine every page of this book: I am grateful for all your edits and recommendations! You encouraged me to share my personal experiences in the book, and *Plan to Be Flexible* is so much better for it. Thank you, thank you.

To those wonderful homeschool moms who continue to strengthen me on my journey: Your stories and advice are the God-given balm for those days when I am tired and doubting. Thank you for your inspiration and leadership.

To Annabelle Tague: thank you for your mad proofreading skills. You have a wonderfully bright future ahead in journalism!

To Cassie Lee: once again, your photos are extraordinary! Thank you for our fun afternoon of photos, pizza and pool play.

To Sharon Marta: you made my book look beautiful! You have given your time and talents over and over to me, and I am so thankful. May the Kingdom of God be blessed by your incredible flair for design.

To my four beautiful children who give me lots to write about: How I treasure each of you and am thrilled to watch you grow! You are each extraordinary people and, as a result, I know your lives for God will be anything but ordinary. I will forever be cheering for you! I love you and am privileged to be called your mom.

To my precious TDK, my constant and my faithful: You have walked with me through every hill and valley of our homeschool journey. I'm so grateful for your listening ear, godly wisdom and servant heart. I could not live this life without you, my wonderful husband and confidante. I love you.

To the Lord Jesus who has not only created me in His image, but who has blessed me with an incredible life here on earth and an indescribably wonderful eternal life ahead: You birthed this book in me, and gave me every single word. Time and time again you proved your faithfulness by providing the examples, the stories and the wisdom. I am honored and exceedingly humbled to be used by you. My sincere prayer is that what's contained in these pages will change lives and bring you all the glory and honor for it.

To the Lord Jesus Christ, who teaches this student every day

CONTENTS

INTRODUCTION:

Happy Homeschool Days Are Ahead!

This book is for the planners out there: those homeschool moms who, like me, love the beauty of a well-ordered day. It's also for those women who are **not** planners by nature but who long to be more organized.

But mostly, this book is for those women (planners or non-planners) who have tried over and over to organize their homeschool days and have felt like an utter failure as they watched their well-laid plans fall to pieces. Those moms who've spent hours on intricate lesson plans only to see a child say, "Do we *have* to do this…?" Moms who have woken up to a house full of runny-nosed, coughing children who need more of a mommy than a teacher that day. My guess is if you've been homeschooling for more than two minutes you can relate (and you can fill in your own situations).

This book was born out of my own tears and endless trial and error. I have tried many systems and schedules and have found myself completely frustrated that each new "miracle" method didn't work long-term.

My days were not organized, no matter how much I tried to make them that way. If I did find a method that worked, it seemed like it was *too* rigid. The kids quickly tired of a strict routine (and frankly, so did I). Alternatively, our planned schoolwork sometimes didn't fit perfectly in the time constraints we'd created, and therefore had to be added to the next day's work. Either way, we'd all end up frustrated and irritated at each other by the end of the day.

Was it the curriculum that wasn't working? Yes, I discovered that sometimes a fresh new curriculum helped. Did I need to change how I presented some of the information and introduce new teaching methods? I did that, and it helped a little too.

However, the biggest change came when I realized that my desire to have everything perfectly planned out was the true source of our frustration. **I'd been holding on so tight to my need for a specific schedule that I'd fallen into the habit of letting anger, frustration and a "just get it done" attitude become a part of our days.** Those incredibly frustrating days had become more the rule than the exception and homeschooling had become a burden.

I had to ask myself: Was school really fun...for me or the kids? Where was the exploration, the joy of learning? It wasn't happening when I felt like a drill sergeant instead of a servant-leader to my kids. I wanted us to have the freedom to explore a topic further and to let them express what they'd been learning in their own unique style; but how was that to happen within a schedule? And how could I make sure that what we were doing every day was in line with our original intentions for homeschooling?

With four kids to teach (plus my roles in running the home, loving my husband, maintaining family relationships, developing friendships with other women, serving at the church, etc.) I knew that organization was essential to survival, but I didn't want to sacrifice the joy of learning (and family relationships) for a rigid schedule.

Was there a way to combine good organization (even planning a year or several months in advance) with free-flowing, student-directed learning—all while still meeting our big-picture homeschooling goals—I wondered? **I sure hoped so.**

This is my journey of discovering that way of schooling—a way to satisfy both my type-A planner personality and my house full of curious, ever-evolving, sometimes-unpredictable students. It is my explanation of **how to put together an organized schedule that accomplishes our big-picture homeschooling goals and leaves room for real-life learning (and *real-life*).**

This is the book that I wish someone had written for me, especially when I was first starting out.

It's not a 10-step method to a perfectly planned schedule (although we will talk about how to do yearly, and weekly planning). Nor is it a listing of the "correct" methods in which to school (however, I will share what works for us).

Instead, it's meant to help you develop a plan that is organized yet flexible for your ever-changing family dynamics.

This book is meant to **challenge some deep concepts about *how* you homeschool**. Concepts like "we are going to do whatever the curriculum tells us, whether we like it or not" that you may have developed to survive those first few years of teaching. The book will also help you consider **your overall goals for educating your children (this year and beyond)** so that you can begin implementing these long-term goals into your everyday schooling. What goals have you set not only for where you want your children to be educationally, but socially and emotionally by the end of the next school year? This will give you guideposts—targets to shoot for—as you determine how to make the most of your time, and thus which elements of your days are non-negotiables.

Lastly, yes, **this book is a compilation of organizational tools and plans** (fellow Type-A women rejoice) so that you can combine your unique goals and homeschool methods into a living and workable daily homeschool schedule.

Also, check out the "Additional Helpful Resources" section in the Appendix. This contains a listing of some of my favorite blogs, tools and resources, including links to some of my blog posts at thevintagecreative.com and to my Pinterest boards (by the way, I am in no way affiliated with links outside of my blog or those within my Pinterest boards).

I am excited to walk on this journey with you as we discover what will not only bring order and peace to our days but will make our teaching time—these precious moments we've been given with our kids!— much more purposeful and productive.

PART 1:

Establish and Refine Goals

CHAPTER 1:

The Finish Line As Daily Guide

The doorbell rang promptly at 8:00 a.m. "Of course she's right on time," I thought to myself, gently sliding the now-dozing baby off my chest and onto the bed next to me.

I rubbed my eyes after the long night with my sleepless newborn and then began the painful process of slowly easing myself off my bed, the week-old Cesarean stitches still angry and sore.

"Miss Marli's here! Miss Marli's here!" the children chorused through the house, all running in merriment to the front door.

"Mom, can we open the door?" my oldest excitedly called up the stairs to me.

"Sure," I managed weakly, glad to not have to hustle myself down the stairs to open it myself.

The door creaked open and I heard a familiar, "Hey guys!"

Marli, an eighteen-year-old homeschooler from our church, had known almost all of my kids since they were infants. As our pastor's daughter and the eldest of six kids, we trusted her implicitly and were thrilled when she'd agreed to help out a few days a week after the birth of our fourth baby.

She embraced each of my kids with a big hug and a few excited greetings. Then suddenly her voice got a little quieter. "Is your momma upstairs with the new baby?"

The kids nodded, grabbed her hand and beckoned her to, "Come see! Come see!"

They bounded up the stairs toward my closed bedroom door, Marli in tow. My daughter ran down the hall and loudly grabbed the door handle, eager to show her friend the tiny new treasure that lay inside.

"Oh! Shhh…" Marli said gently. "Better not open the door. The baby might be sleeping."

By this time I'd hobbled to the door and opened it myself. "Good morning, Marli," I whispered quietly, managing a smile.

"Good morning, Mrs. Kazsuk!" she said in a cheery whisper. She glanced at the bed where my nine-pound bundle lay, swaddled as snugly as a Christmas present. She also noticed my bloodshot eyes and how I looked…well, probably not how she recognized me on a Sunday morning. Though she'd never spent all night with a screaming baby as I had the night before, I saw compassion cross her face and spill out into her words. "How can I best help you?" she asked softly.

Tears filled my eyes. I was so grateful that she'd had the sense to ask. "I really just need to sleep," I managed. "I had a really rough night."

She nodded empathetically. "He looks like he's sleeping now. Can I take him for you so that you can sleep without worrying about him?"

4

Yes, that was exactly what I'd wanted but was too uncertain to ask. After all, she also had my three other kids to watch!

"That would be wonderful, Marli. Are you sure you can manage?" I said.

"Sure, no problem, Mrs. Kazsuk. Anything I can do to help," she said, quietly tiptoeing into the room and carefully cradling the contented infant. She left the room, making a soothing "shhh..." sound to the other kids who were following behind her like ducks in a row.

I closed the door behind her, my heart filled with thankfulness that God had allowed this time in Marli's busy schedule so she could help our family through this transition.

At eighteen, Marli had not only graduated high school but had completed her Bachelor's degree. Fresh out of school, she was just about to embark on another exciting project: illustrating a series of children's books for a well-known author. Clearly she was extremely intelligent, talented and going places.

For many years I had watched Marli and her siblings grow in poise and character. While I knew these were not perfect kids (her mom and I are friends and have swapped stories), clearly there was something right going on in this homeschooled home.

These kids—and so many other homeschooling kids I knew—were inquisitive yet respectful, spoke intelligently with both their peers and with adults, and possessed a certain confidence that was neither prideful nor cocky. They were quick to serve, happy to help and, as a result, were trusted with responsibilities far beyond their years.

Behind these capable young homeschool kids were their intentional parents: the quiet heroes that had planned, prayed, sacrificed and given of themselves day in and day out in unseen and laudable ways. These parents too were not perfect, yet God had used their best efforts to guide these kids down the right path.

It was obvious that these parents had made deliberate (perhaps difficult) choices in guiding their children. The fruit in these kids' lives was not the result of chance but of specific plans and goals (and lots of prayer).

While each family's path was unique, it was evident that they had begun (and continued) their homeschooling journey with the end in mind. They had dreamt big dreams for their kids, prayed for God's direction and guidance, and outlined specific goals for how to make those dreams a reality. Like a marathon runner with the finish line in mind, they'd diligently plugged away at their big picture objectives, trusting God to fulfill His plan.

Where Are You Headed?

It may sound basic, but **developing an effective homeschool schedule starts with the finish line in mind.**

Twenty years from now, what do you want your children to have gained from their homeschool education? What are your long-term goals for homeschooling?

My guess is that your goals go much deeper than just teaching the multiplication table or the life cycle of a butterfly. Honestly, your kids could probably pick those things up over at your local public school.

So, in a nutshell, *why* are you homeschooling, and *what* do you hope to accomplish?

Some of the reasons *why* you've chosen homeschooling could include:

- One-on-one teaching

- Customized curriculum

- Teaching that moves at your child's pace

- Interest-led learning

- Separation from negative peer influences

- Ability to teach certain topics from a biblical perspective

- Time together as a family

What you hope to give your child through homeschooling might include:

- A biblically-focused worldview

- A well-rounded, college-prep education

- Strong relationships within the family unit

- A deep, growing faith in Christ

- Strong moral character

- Leadership skills

- Ability to work well in groups

If you have never thought through your motivations and goals behind homeschooling, I'd highly encourage you to pray, consult your spouse and deeply consider what God wants you to focus on during these precious homeschool years.

Dream about the type of education you'd like your kids to have. Don't stifle yourself. Don't allow your past mistakes or a child's previous challenges limit what you can dream up. We are starting new here, with a clean slate.

While some educational goals may be the same for all your students, don't be afraid to create individual student goals too. Consider each child's unique personality and abilities. When do you see them soar? What makes their heart sing? What challenges do you want to help them overcome? What kind of goals have they set for themselves (in the near or distant future) and how can you help them achieve those goals?

I love the mental picture of a child as a rocket and a parent as the launching pad and ground crew. We parents are given the first 18 years to shape the future trajectory of our little "rocket." What will we use to fuel up our kids so they can blast off toward their intended destiny with power and conviction? It's not our job to aim our child

8

where we want them to go, but instead, through the wisdom of God, help the child discern his natural talents and interests and then help point him in that direction. It is our job as parents to prepare, guide and to lead them on their journey.

Schooling is how we get them off the ground and airborne. Schooling is the fuel that sets them soaring toward the incredible plans God has dreamt for them.

Relationships, Character Building And Real-World Learning

My, how my schooling goals have changed since I first started out!

I shared previously about the number of homeschoolers that my husband and I have encountered. These kids—well-manned, highly inquisitive young people who were excitedly pursuing God's purpose for their lives—were the reason we initially decided to homeschool. Whatever was in the homeschool Kool-Aid, we wanted our kids to drink it!

Education and book-learning have always been high priorities in my life. Growing up, I loved school and got excellent grades. So, even though I had gone to public school (and didn't know any homeschoolers during my time in school) I was convinced that I would have *no problem* teaching my kids at home! It was just imparting educational knowledge to my own dear children, right? Armed with a good curriculum and a love to learn, I felt well prepared to give my kids the best educational experience possible.

With visions of national spelling bees dancing in my head, I saw my ultimate homeschooling goal as raising ambitious, high-achieving children that would be successful and happy in whatever God called them to do.

Then one day I asked a dear friend—who also happened to be a highly respected homeschooling mom—why she and her husband decided to teach their kids at home.

Honestly, her answer shocked me… and changed my life.

Focus #1: Building Relationships

"Alicia," she began, "We have only eighteen years to impact a child's life before they are turned loose to the world. Those precious years are foundational for the rest of the child's life, and as parents we need to make the most of every moment. I am not willing to give up eight hours a day, five days a week to someone else to make *their* impact on *my* child."

She went on to explain that "making an impact" went way beyond just teaching school subjects. Although she did her best to give her kids a well-rounded education, she stated **that wasn't the main goal of her homeschool.** Rather, she said that **"school" was merely a conduit** for building family relationships and thus the **relationships built during "school time"** *won her the opportunity* **to speak into her children's lives about deeper issues.** Building friendship, trust and mutual respect between family members were her ultimate goals because these opened the doors to true discipleship and lasting connections with her kids.

10

Focus #2: Character Development

Not only was homeschooling an incredible conduit for relationship building, she said, the hours and days spent together in the classroom were incredible modeling grounds for moral and character development and for Christian discipleship.

She explained that teaching character development went much further than simply making kids memorize character traits. Since more is "caught than taught" when it comes to parenting, character development started with an honest assessment of the parent's own moral and character development, she said. This takes time and lots of discipline but the benefits (both for the parent and the child) far exceeded any cost.

Focus #3: Real-World Preparation

My friend also talked—a lot!—about how she wanted to prepare her kids for the "real world."

My first response to this was, "OK…I am doing this…I am teaching my kids how to read, how to do math. Check that box!"

But it turns out she was also talking about a wide variety of things. There were things that adults needed to know (that they *might* pick up in a classroom): how to take notes, how to prepare for a job interview, how to solve problems in a group, how to balance a checkbook, etc. There were also things that adults needed to know (but that they *wouldn't* learn in a typical classroom): how to do laundry, how to cook for a dozen people, how to clean a house, how to be a good host, etc. And of course there were the deeper questions

11

of life (that many adults are still trying to figure out): "Who am I?" "What is my purpose?" "Why was I made this way?"

Clearly, preparing a child for the real world—in the way she was speaking of—went way beyond teaching reading, writing and arithmetic. That day I realized that God had built amazing opportunities into homeschooling—opportunities that, frankly, just weren't present in other schooling methods.

Are Daily Activities In Line With Homeschooling Goals?

Yes, that conversation opened new doors on the possibilities of homeschooling. But unfortunately, it didn't change how I homeschooled each day. Why? **Because I'd not realigned my goals—and subsequently my daily schedule—to this way of thinking.**

I still found myself pushing the kids through lesson plans and a strict, hour-by-hour routine that blessed quantifiable amounts of bookwork over the development of deep, lasting relationships. Mastering a subject (often in the way the curriculum considered "mastering") was our ultimate goal. I saw some bonding occurring between the kids and I, but how deep were those bonds? Were they deep enough to help us navigate the potentially tricky future waters of adolescence and beyond? And most importantly, were the kids being drawn into a relationship with Christ after seeing my daily actions as a Christ-follower?

Finally, several years later, I found myself—and my students—burnt out on school. They were tired of being "forced" to learn—and I was incredibly tired of "convincing" them that they needed to learn.

My husband and I didn't want to throw in the towel on our homeschooling experiment. We still felt it was the best way to educate our kids.

But clearly, some things needed to change in our daily routine. We needed to come up with some new goals for how to structure our school, and then to allow those goals to redefine our day-to-day activities.

With the end in mind, we realized that we needed to:

- Clearly define our homeschooling objectives (both our overall goals and any specific goals for each individual child); and

- Make an action plan for implementing these objectives. We prayed that a change in the focus of school activities would result in a change in attitudes regarding school (for both me and the kids).

Here's what we came up with.

Why We Homeschool:

- Customized learning that focuses on our children's individual learning styles and talents

- Concepts are learned at each child's speed

- The option of which subjects to cover (and not cover) based on child's needs or maturity

- Character training/teaching about biblical concepts interwoven into everyday lessons

- Spiritual disciplines more easily introduced into daily activities

- School calendar formulated to dates that work best for our family's needs

- Free time in our days for relaxation, family fun and bonding (instead of time spent driving from school to school)

- Strong parent-child bonds and sibling-to-sibling bonds more easily developed

- Removal from negative influences and peer pressure during the early impressionable years

- Difficult subjects discussed at the appropriate age for each individual child

- Difficult subject matter presented from a biblical worldview and within the context of our strong parent-child bond.

- Real world learning incorporated into lesson plans and practiced in daily routines

- Field trips and "outside the book" learning available as we see fit

What We Hope To Give Our Kids:

- A close relationship with Christ and a complete picture of what it means to be a Christ-follower

- A strong moral character rooted in biblical integrity, perseverance and humility

- A direction and purpose for where God has called them in life

- A deep relationship and connection with us, their parents

- Rich, ever-growing relationships with their siblings

- Real-world knowledge in everything from how to cook and do laundry to how to resolve conflicts and work with those that are "different" from them

- A comprehensive, well-rounded education in the traditional school subjects

- A life-long love of learning

(Note: These are our corporate homeschool goals, but we also included some specifics goals for a few of our children. For example, one of our children has

some social challenges, so, under "What We Hope to Give Our Kids," we gave this child the additional goal of "the ability to interact well with others, to accurately assess other's feelings and to develop strong friendships." If our children were older and were confident in their future career aspirations, we could also develop additional individual goals that would prepare them for that specific future.)

How did these goals change our daily routine?

Our school now provides a high-quality academic experience *within the context of the outlined objectives.* A rigorous and engaging academic atmosphere is still high priority, but it is no longer *top* priority. **Science, History, Math, Reading—these are the** *methods and practicums* **for learning character development, study skills and real-world preparation.**

This means that I am now more concerned that my son knows *how* **to find the answers to his questions** about the Civil War than to memorize the dates and major battles of this conflict. This also means that I want him **to be inspired by the great people of history**, and to learn from their successes and failures as he travels on his path toward being a world changer himself.

The knowledge and the subsequent school activities have a deeper purpose: what can the student learn about God from this? What new study or organizational skills can they acquire from the assignment? And how can examining this topic lead to a deeper understanding of Christ—his creation and his plan for mankind?

What has been the result of these changes?

While I would love to tell you that our homeschool days are a picture of utter perfection, I must admit that there are still mornings where my kids wake up and aren't excited to do school. There are still times when I have to summon my inner motivational speaker to convince my kids that, yes, we need to write that outline or finish those math problems.

But things have *dramatically improved* for the better.

Thankfully, our tough days are few and far between. I am learning every day how to let go of my ideas of "how" they need to be taught and instead allowing them to discover the information and respond to it in their own unique way. I've found ways to make school fun and interesting. Our relationships have dramatically improved. I'm learning to slow down, to relax and to enjoy my kids through this process.

And what's ironic is that **I feel like they've gained more book knowledge than ever before**! I am shocked at all that they have learned! And I'm proud to watch them embrace learning and to happily dig deep into subjects.

Action Plan:

Before you go any farther in this book, I challenge you to deeply examine your homeschool's big-picture goals.

1. **First and foremost, pray.** Ask God for help and for His wisdom in figuring out an overall action plan that works. He longs to give your family a purposeful and powerful homeschooling experience.

2. **Ask yourself the big questions**: "Why has our family chosen to homeschool?" and "What are our overall goals in homeschooling?" Write these as corporate homeschooling goals for all of your kids. Also write down any individual goals you may have for a specific child. On his graduation day, what do you want to have imparted to your child?

Stay at this step as long as you need to! Just like building a home starts with a solid foundation, take the time necessary to establish goals and set big picture plans for your school. The success of your homeschool schedule (and of course, your homeschool!) depends on this critical step.

CHAPTER 2:

What's Working... (And What's Not) (Part 1)

If you've set goals in the past and accomplished them all perfectly, you have my permission to skip this chapter (and the next one).

For the rest of us mortals, let's talk about the ugly side of goal-making.

Goals can be beautiful, precious things—lofty plans we make *before* we set foot on the path. They can seem easy—too easy—to fulfill. They lure us in with their wonderful promises ("if you work out and lose 20 pounds, you can drop two dress sizes!"). We convince ourselves that if we only meet these goals then our lives will be truly happy and complete.

We make our plans on the mountaintops, but oh, we must still trudge through the valleys. While joys do exist in the valleys of everyday homeschool life, the valleys can also be filled with bad attitudes, ineffective curriculums and overcrowded schedules.

Otherwise known as "stuff that's *not* working in your school."

Thankfully our homeschooling cycles come equipped with a summer break. This is our opportunity to climb back up the mountain, breathe the fresh air and grab a new focus for the year ahead. We can revisit our goals, determine what is working (and what is not) and continue back down the mountain with a new game plan. I'd highly encourage

19

you to **do this every year** as a healthy part of your homeschool routine.

But sometimes we get so off-track from our goals that **we have to climb up the mountain much earlier than the planned summer break**. We even may have to climb up there several times in a single school year. Life may have smacked us around a bit, or a child might be going through an especially difficult season, and we just need to be able to stand back and take a look at the big picture. We can't be afraid to step away from what's not working and take a hard look at what's causing all the frustration.

My Lowest Point

In early 2010 I found myself burnt out. I was tired of the endless pushing through the curriculum and fights each day to get school done. I felt like no matter how hard I'd tried, my children were still not the happy homeschool kids I'd wanted them to be. School became a burden and learning lacked joy — for me and my kids.

At that time we were schooling under a local public charter school and were required to meet with an educational specialist (ES) from the school every five weeks to assess our progress.

I clearly remember one meeting around that time. We were sitting outside a local coffee shop with the ES, school papers in hand. My students were *not* engaged in our conversation but were extremely distracted by the birds flying around the tables that were gathering bits of muffins and other pastries left behind by other patrons. As the meeting progressed, my frustration level increased higher and higher as I listened to my kids' responses to her questions about what they'd been learning: "Huh?" "I don't know." "I don't remember." They continued to look everywhere but at her and it was all that I could do to keep them in their seats.

Toward the end of our conversation I finally gave up and let the kids leave the table and chase the birds around the courtyard instead. I was embarrassed by my students' lack of attention and lack of knowledge. **I'd been working incredibly hard**—perhaps harder than ever before—week after week to diligently teach my kids, **and yet here was the extremely unsatisfying result of all my labor.**

I didn't expect them to perform like trained monkeys, but it was obvious that something wasn't working in our schooling. I'd seen further evidence of this in the previous weeks when I'd spent an inordinate amount of effort barking at my squirmy boys to "sit down" "pay attention" and "finish the workbook" while they moaned and groaned.

It was an understatement to say that this driven perfectionist felt shamed and humbled by homeschooling. And now my failures were evident to others outside our home (a school official, no less!).

While the kids chased the birds a few tables away, the ES leaned in closer to me and asked me if everything was alright at home. She said that I seemed to be stressed and that my tone with my kids had been "sharp."

Could this meeting get any worse? I thought. *Now not only am I a poor homeschooler but a terrible parent as well?*

Tears began flowing down my cheeks. "School has not been going so well," I finally managed. "I'm working so hard and we're doing all the assignments, I swear..." My voice trailed off.

The ES, herself a homeschool mom, sat silent for a moment and then said, "Maybe you need to step back and re-examine how you're doing things."

Yeah, duh! I wanted to say. *Did she really think I hadn't thought of that?* I'd spent each evening with my husband venting about my school frustrations and we'd yet to come up with workable solutions. The big questions were of course was what to change? And what to change it to?

I left that meeting feeling utterly defeated, frustrated and at my wits' end. I wasn't ready to throw in the towel but had no idea what to do next.

Over the next few days I spoke with several veteran homeschool moms about their times of greatest frustration. Their advice was unanimous: I needed to back way off with school.

"It doesn't matter that you are in the middle of the school year," they explained. "You don't want to hurt your relationships with your kids or destroy their love of learning. That is far more important than completing the expected tasks and satisfying school requirements."

I have to admit that I didn't completely agree (I was still convinced that book knowledge was the main goal of homeschooling) but I trusted these women who'd been on the path much longer. I began the extremely humbling task of ceasing our homeschool routine.

For the next few weeks, I nursed my wounds and cried out in prayer. I was angry and disillusioned. Not only did I need direction, but clearly God needed to heal some deep hurts and disappointments inside of me.

Time passed, and I began slowly introducing school again through games. Monopoly, Bananagrams and card games like Go Fish were brought out of our board game cabinet and into the core of our days. We spent a lot of time outside in our backyard and at the park playing. We read a lot (not "school-ish" books, mind you, but old family favorites that we'd read over and over).

I felt like I was re-introducing learning to my kids...and to myself. It was as if we'd had a cancer removed, and were now in the hospital healing and recovering.

I found a math curriculum that was completely workbook-free (Math had been one of our biggest battlegrounds and I think my forced time in the workbook had made this subject extremely unappealing for my kids). Very, very slowly we began working through a few sections with each child. **On days when they could "sniff" that we were "doing school" and began to show signs of resistance, I backed way off again.**

It was a slow and painful recovery but oh, I learned so much. Instead of forcing a "correct" method or style of learning on my kids (no matter how good it had worked for someone else), **I learned to trust my kids' behavior and their responses to how I'd been teaching them**. These were unique creations of God. How could I expect a prescribed formula or curriculum to address and meet their one-of-a-kind needs?

I also learned to respect their viewpoint and to value our relationship above any school task that needed to be completed. I learned to sense when I was offering them **a healthy challenge that would stretch and grow their skills, and when I was just pushing them and needed to relax**. It was a major turning point in my skills as a teacher, and as a mom.

Making Your Own Assessments

Whether we're going through a difficult homeschool time or it's just time for an annual check-up, **we need to be honest about where our students (or where we) are, and then be prepared to make whatever changes necessary to make school engaging, productive and effective**. Regardless of when or how often, it's critical to weigh the current health of our school against our ultimate homeschool motivations and goals.

At the end of the school year (or whenever your homeschool needs a fresh start) take some time to examine the key components of your homeschool. Pray for great insight and knowledge into each child's current educational experience. Ask your spouse for his take on what he sees as working (and not working) in your school.

Specifically speaking, what should you consider? To get your wheels turning, here are a few questions (the Appendix has a more comprehensive list):

About The Curricula/Learning Style:

1. Is real learning happening here? Do you see evidences of the child not only understanding the concepts but applying them in other school subjects and even in everyday conversation?

2. Do you battle with a child to complete a particular subject, and do you believe that the curricula may be partially to blame?

3. Do the curricula allow for the type of learning that you've chosen for your homeschool (for example, interest-led learning, literature-based learning, etc.)?

About The Student(s):

1. What are his areas of weakness and areas of strength? What can you do to strengthen the weak areas?

2. Are there core skills that you want him to learn by this time next year?

3. Does he need assistance from outside sources (such as a tutor)?

About The School Structure/Schedule:

1. Does the time spent on school work for your students' needs and for the entire family schedule?

2. Will there be an expected life change next year (for example, a new baby, a planned move, a part-time job for mom) that will require a change in the annual homeschool schedule or in the daily hours of schooling?

3. Should you consider adding additional out-of-the-home learning experiences, such as sports, clubs, or co-op teaching classes? Or do you participate in those experiences now and plan on eliminating them next year?

About The Teacher:

1. Are there things about your teaching style that you'd like to change?

2. Do you regularly exhibit the classroom behavior that you want your kids to have?

3. Would you choose you as your teacher?

Make a commitment to do whatever it takes—reading books, talking to other moms, going to a homeschool conference—to discover solutions to whatever issues are present. This can be the hardest step, but God will be faithful to provide real answers to your issues.

Action Plan:

1. Take an afternoon and think through your school's current status. Using the questions listed in the chapter (and additional questions in the Appendix), take an honest assessment of your school, your students and your teaching. Are you still on track with the ultimate homeschooling goals you've established?

2. What are the biggest issues in your homeschool?

3. Is the curriculum still working for your students? Do you need to examine new teaching styles and methods?

4. Pray for great insight into your homeschool's unique issues. Write down what comes to mind, or what God reveals.

CHAPTER 3:

What's Working...And What's Not (Part 2)

Next, I suggest you do something radical: Ask your kids' opinion about homeschooling. **What do they like about school? If they were the teacher, what would they do differently?**

Now you may be saying, "What?! Should they have that much input in how our school is run?!"

Absolutely!

While it certainly would be easier if we were raising autonomous robots, the fact is that our students are uniquely designed. They have strengths and weaknesses (those that are part of their personality and those that are present just for this life stage) and this affects how they respond to a teaching style or method.

We can make all the plans we want, but **if those plans aren't working for our children, then what's the point?** As parents we can ascertain a lot of what's going on in our child, but only *they* fully know what's happening in that gray matter.

When a manager gives an employee an annual review, doesn't the manager ask the employee to give a self-evaluation—a review of where the employee feels he is being successful (and where he needs to make changes)? The employee is often also asked to share any suggestions he has to improve the workplace or to improve productivity. Ideally, it's a two-sided conversation between the employer and the employee, with both giving input to determine the best possible working environment.

Shouldn't we give our kids the same respect and opportunity for input? It is their schooling, after all.

The End-Of-The-Year Date

Each year, around the end of May, I get to plan one of my favorite school days: our teacher-child date.

The kids *love* this special time with mom, and so do I! It's the perfect way to celebrate all the wonderful things they've learned this year and to verbally affirm how much they have grown.

It's also the perfect opportunity to get their honest assessment of last year's homeschool successes and failures.

Here are some suggestions on how to conduct your own special date with your student(s).

Invitation. About a week before the date, put together a fun invite for each child. You can go hog-wild here (if you want): a computer designed invitation, a handwritten invite, an email, a card, a scavenger hunt, a note with a picture of the child—you name it. Include the day, time and location of the date. If the child is older, you might also list some questions for them to consider as preparation for your time together.

Some years my invites have been fancier than others (depending on my time and creativity level)! **One year I invited my boys to their end-of-the-year dates via two cleverly packaged gift cards.** I purchased a gift card for the approximate cost of the date (I told them later that I wanted them to feel like "they" were the ones "paying"). I grabbed an actual plastic cup from the coffee shop along with a lid, straw and logo-themed napkins. I scrunched the napkins up inside the see-through cup so that it looked like the cup was filled with a yummy frozen beverage. I stuck the gift card in the middle of the napkins, put on the lid and stuck a straw through. Then, on the side of the cup I used a black permanent marker to write the actual invitation, listing the date and time. I did something similar for an invitation to a frozen yogurt place (filling an empty yogurt container with logo-themed napkins and the gift card, and writing the invitation in black permanent marker on the side of the container). Both were a hit!

Location. First and foremost, choose a place that the child would enjoy (hint: *that place* they keep asking you about!).

My five-year-old daughter is *in love* with our local cupcakery and gets googly-eyed when we drive by (I think it's all the pink frills and frosting...I get a sugar high just walking in the place!). So it's a no-brainer where her end-of-the-year-date will be this year.

For your child, maybe it's a frozen yogurt place, sitting on a bench at the park, time at the beach or other scenic location, or even a special "tea time" in the backyard. Wherever you choose, make sure the location allows for conversation and possibly has a table or desk so you can share papers and projects together as you talk.

Preparation. Make sure you've thought through your own assessment of the school year, particularly in the areas involving this student. Write down your thoughts and bring them with you. If there are issues of concern (and those issues can be seen in his work), bring samples so that he can see it first-hand. In addition, bring samples that demonstrate his hard work and be ready to praise all the wonderful things he has accomplished.

Most of all, bathe the meeting time in prayer. Ask God for ideas in how to steer the conversation; a spirit of openness (for both you and your child) that respects the other's point of view; ears to pick up on any potentially hidden frustrations; and wisdom for coming up with solutions to issues presented.

Agenda. This can be as formal or informal as you feel necessary. For example, you may decide to talk about one subject at a time or about overall topics that need to be addressed (or a combo of both). Here are some potential conversation starters:

- What was his favorite project or activity, and why?

- Ask him to list 3-5 concepts he learned this year. What does he remember most?

- Is there something specific that he would like to learn more about next year?

- Which subjects does he need to focus on next year?

- Are there current learning concepts that he doesn't understand?

- When and where does he feel he does the best work (a specific time of day or location)?

- What are his strongest subjects?

- Does he like the curriculum? Is the information presented in an interesting way?

- And (here's a convicting one!): would he recommend his school to others as a great place to learn? Why or why not?

Atmosphere. Praise, praise, praise the child! Although some potentially tough topics may come up, keep the tone of the conversation light and mostly celebratory. You do want to get his feedback about the year, and he will be much more apt to give it in a welcoming atmosphere.

Also, be committed to truly listen and validate any suggestions they give. I bring a notebook with me to write down any ideas (this helps convince them that their input is being taken seriously).

Of course, the process of getting a child's input can be much more informal than what I've outlined here. It may simply happen through a casual dinner conversation, or while waiting in line at an amusement park! There's no special formula.

Assessing And Filtering Their Input

Getting a child's input is critical, but as a staunch advocate of parent-led (instead of child-run) households, I do have to add three caveats.

First, the **weight of a child's input varies based on their age and maturity**. A mature 13-year-old's opinion should obviously be given much more consideration than a kindergartner's.

Second, it's also assumed that any seriously considered **suggestions still line up under the overarching goals of your homeschool, and of the laws of your state**. These two are non-negotiables.

Third, the **parents' opinions should be given the highest weight of all**. As full-fledged adults (charged with complete responsibility for the minor child) we make the final call on any changes that are made. We are the "employers," so to speak, in the employer/employee relationship. Even though employees are usually given the opportunity to share input, ultimately the employer has the responsibility to make sure that the company's goals are met.

It's important that kids understand this concept when asked to offer their input. My kids know that their opinion is valued and important. However they also know that, as they describe it, "If we each have one vote about something, Mommy and Daddy have ten votes!"

As long as these guidelines are not jeopardized, I highly encourage you to consider a child's suggestions.

Dealing With "Childish" Input

But I know what's coming, you say. My child's "input" will simply be "I don't want to do math" or "I don't like school at all."

Yes, probably so! Expect some of that! This is a normal response for a kid on this subject. I mean, if you were an eight-year-old boy, wouldn't you rather build forts and play LEGOs than learn about the basics of English Grammar?

It's important that we listen to our kid's suggestions, even if they are...*ahem*, childish. Respect is a two-way street, and we can't demand it from our kids if we aren't willing to offer it ourselves.

But how can we marry their (perhaps unrealistic) expectations with the realities of what needs to be accomplished? While there's no perfect answer to this question, I'd say that honest communication (and an open mind) goes a long way.

Here's an example. When asked his input about Algebra and World History, twelve-year-old Bobby says that he hates both subjects and would much rather go surfing instead.

"Ummm...OK..." is your response. "Let's talk about that further. Why don't you like these subjects?"

He shares that he's bored of always writing a three-point essay for History (and that Algebra puts him to sleep).

Since History and Algebra are state-mandated subjects, Bobby must have them as part of his school day. However, there's room for adaptation.

Instead of always writing an essay for History, what if he switched it up sometimes and created a poster board for a specific History topic? Or what if he designed a video or PowerPoint presentation to outline what he's learned? Maybe he can focus on a specific aspect of history that he finds interesting (such as a historical figure or a specific event). How can the subject be taught (and the information expressed) in ways that he would find more interesting?

Thankfully, there are oodles of books (and blogs) dedicated to making history come alive. Some curriculums like *Tapestry of Grace* and Diana Waring's *History Revealed* Curriculum contain fascinating activities and projects for each weekly history topic. Pinterest is also an excellent place to look for ideas. You can follow my "Homeschooling—History Activities and Projects" board, or simply type in a topic in the Pinterest search box and see what others are doing.

And in the case of Algebra, perhaps he can try a different Math curriculum or method. There are so many out-of-the-workbook ideas out there. Or maybe he needs additional help from a tutor. Or would he benefit from doing math first thing in the morning (instead of the afternoon, like he'd been doing it)? These are all points of dialog to have with your student. Back and forth conversation (and opportunities for trial and error) are essential here.

And yes…what about surfing? Maybe you could make time in the schedule for surfing or other activities your student enjoys. Perhaps participation in these activities could be conditional on him having the right attitude and giving 100 percent in his regular subjects. Of course participation in the activity *at all* is up to you the parent. However, by allowing time for these "non-schoolbook" activities, it might demonstrate that his input is valued and that you do want to make time for things that he enjoys.

36

Dealing With No Input

On the opposite spectrum, you might have a child that gives *no input or suggestions* when asked about school.

This is a plausible scenario, especially if you've never given them a forum for input before! Some kids are shy about giving their opinion. Or, more commonly, a child may just have never thought about the details of what they do or don't like about school.

A few years ago, I discovered that sometimes kids (especially the "good," well-manned kids we are attempting to raise) can be experts at camouflaging their feelings about a particular school subject.

One of my kids clearly disliked our math program. His poor attitude and my constant nagging were dead giveaways. I also noted that he just wasn't understanding the concepts. So, when it came time for our end-of-the-year assessment, **it was a no-brainer that we needed to look for a new math curriculum for him.**

However, I was surprised to discover that my other son greatly disliked math too! I would have never guessed this since he dutifully did his assignments and seemed to understand the subject matter.

I think he didn't really know how to verbalize what he was thinking until I directly asked him in an end-of-the-year evaluation. So once I discovered that he too hated math, we talked about why things weren't working, and determined a new learning style and curriculum that might work better for him.

Putting It All Together

Gathering input can be wonderfully informative...and emotionally exhausting! Sometimes instead of clearing up issues, hearing additional viewpoints present new problems to solve.

Take time to digest all that you discussed with your students before making concrete decisions about next year. If additional conversation is needed on a topic, continue that conversation with the child before making changes.

You may also find yourself with more research to do: Is different curriculum needed? Does a subject need to be taught in a new way? Do resources for a new subject need to be discovered?

Although it may seem cumbersome to assess and analyze your homeschool in this way, the information gathered plays a critical role in determining specific goals for next year. Armed with the big picture goals for your school (and with an understanding of what's working and not working currently), you can accurately define next year's goals.

Action Plan:

1. Prepare for and host an end-of-the-year date with your student(s). Come armed with a celebratory spirit and an open heart to listen to their input.

2. Gather up all the information that you learned. Based on your assessments and the student(s)' input, what changes need to be made? What new resources do you need to discover?

CHAPTER 4:

Determine This Year's Goals

"Tree houses?" I asked, surprised.

"Yeah, tree houses," my oldest son replied. "I think it would be cool to learn about how to build a tree house."

My son and I were on our annual "End of the Year Date," talking about what he wanted to learn about next year.

Hmmm… I thought of our postage-stamp-sized backyard and the definite *lack* of large trees with sturdy trunks. *Not a promising haven for tree-house-building.*

Next I thought of a recent conversation I'd had with my husband (while he was sweating profusely in an attempt to build a "simple" bookshelf) where he made me promise not to ever, *ever* ask him to do a woodworking project again. *Strike two on the tree house idea.*

I shared my initial thoughts with my son (*why tree house probably equals no dice*). Still he persisted.

He showed me pictures of several extravagant structures, some with glass windows and slides down the back. These things were amazing masterpieces, many of them clearly *not* "built by kids" as the site claimed (*what moron showed him that site anyway?!*).

He continued to present his case. Not deterred by my "lack of sturdy trees" comment, he walked me outside and explained his vision for cutting into our slope so that the tree house could be somehow built into the side of our hill. "Who needs a tree, Mom?!" my excited future engineer exclaimed. *Well, I think the neighbors who* live *on top of the hill probably prefer we use a tree,* I thought.

Then he told me about how a family we knew had built bookshelves, chairs and even bunk beds right in their own garage. I too loved this family—and had seen their mad skills with a hammer and nails—but at that moment I wanted to disconnect all their power tools and other assorted carpentry thingies.

Then the light went on in my head. Ultimately, it wasn't a fancy tree house that he was after! "Aha! You want to do *woodworking*!" I said.

He gave me a confused look. *The boy doesn't know the term "woodworking,"* I thought. *More evidence that the tree house idea is not a wise one.*

"Woodworking… Carpentry…" I said.

Another blank look.

"You want to make things out of wood," I said finally.

His eyes lit up. "Yes, Mom! That's what I want to do!" he cried.

My homeschool mom brain went into action. Woodworking equaled measuring. Adding. Estimating. Dividing. *What other math skills could I eke out of this?*

I'm sure the state department of education believes that woodworking doesn't hold a hammer to "proper" academic subjects like science and literature. But who knew? Maybe my son would learn a skill that would eventually become his future profession. Maybe one day as a husband he'd find no greater joy than building a bookshelf for his overly ambitious wife. Or maybe he just wanted to bang around with a hammer (as only a nine-year-old boy can do) and make a lot of noise (which was alright too).

Regardless of the reason, that day I said yes to the woodworking idea. **It was important to him, and so it became important to me.**

We agreed that it wasn't going to take the place of our regular school subjects, but **he and I wrote "learning how to build with wood" as one of his learning goals for the following year.**

And that's the next step in our planning process: **crafting annual goals for each child**. This is where you take all the input you've gathered (including the "I want to build a tree house"-type comments), lay them side by side with your big-picture homeschool goals and make some decisions for the upcoming year.

Setting Annual Goals For Each Child

I could make this section of the book really complicated and drawn out, but the bottom line here is you're going to gather up all that you've learned and make a good, old-fashioned list. You can make a fancy list (ooh...spreadsheets...) or a writing-on-a-napkin-type of list. As homeschool moms, we take whatever's in front of us (laptop or

43

dinner plate) when the ideas, inspiration and time come available, right?

First, list out the subjects you plan to cover, making separate columns for each student. Start with the state-mandated staples — math, science, history and the like. Then include any other subjects that help meet your family's big picture homeschool goals (for our family that's "Bible" and "Character Training"), along with specialized subjects or topics for each student (this is where "woodworking" comes in). List sports, music lessons or other activities here as well. Write any notes about each subject such as "need new curriculum," "make a priority next year" or "ready for a challenge."

Next, write some quantifiable objectives for each subject, based on your own analysis of your school (and the feedback you received from your students). This is where you detail exactly what you plan to cover next year. For example, you might write "The Middle Ages, the Renaissance and the Age of Explorers" as a history objective or "making outlines, and writing paragraphs and topical essays" as writing goals. These are the specific topics or tools you want your student(s) to have mastered by the end of the school year. As necessary, further divide these objectives into weekly, quarterly and half-year goals.

At this point, however, try to not get too bogged down in the details. We'll talk in much more detail about establishing a curriculum core and sequencing subject material in Chapter 6.

Suggestions For Setting Objectives

A quick aside here: I highly recommend that you **focus on concepts learned, not curriculum or workbook completion.** In other words, it's much more effective to write "review multiplication facts, learn about fractions and introduce geometry" than to write "finish math workbook 2A and 2B." Yes, write down names of specific curriculum if you know which ones would help meet the targeted objectives. However, I'm suggesting that a student's annual learning goals be tied to actually understanding the material versus simply finishing the book. You may have completed the prescribed curriculum and the student still doesn't understand the concept!

We have to be honest enough in our assessments to sometimes say, "That style or method didn't effectively teach the concept last year. This year, let's learn about this topic again, but take a different approach." This way, **the curriculum becomes the servant to the student's learning needs**, rather than the other way around.

Second, if you have multiple students, I suggest **teaching the same topic to all of the children at the same time**. For example, if you have five children, there's no reason for them to be studying five different history curricula! Why not streamline the process and teach the same history topic to all the different levels at once?

The entire family may learn about the Civil War at the same time, but naturally, **each child will demonstrate what they've learned in different capacities based on their age and grade level.** Students may all learn about Lincoln's assassination, but perhaps a kindergartner colors a picture of Lincoln at Ford Theater (and narrates to you one or two sentences about what happened that fateful day on April 14, 1865 in Washington, D.C.); a third grader composes a sequence of events of that night; a fifth-grader writes a first-person account of the shooting (pretending to be the medical officer that helped the slain president); and a ninth-grader writes a two-page report about the reasons behind the assassination. This teaching style greatly simplifies teaching multiple children, and allows for the entire family to delve deep into a subject together. The *Tapestry of Grace* history curriculum has this concept down pat, offering student activities and projects ranging from lower grammar to high school levels.

There will, of course, be subjects that require different learning levels (math, for example). This is a necessary part of making sure that each student is appropriately challenged. However, if you're teaching multiple students, take advantage of every opportunity to teach the same topic to all the students.

Third, I'd also like to make the case for choosing one subject as the driving force behind the majority of your learning content. Not only does this allow students to really dig deep into a topic, it further simplifies teaching! It's natural to establish learning content around broad subjects like history and science because often learning objectives from several other subjects can be accomplished through one history or science project.

Let me give you an example. We're currently studying World War II as our history topic and the kids are putting together notebooks about each aspect of the war as we study it. A large part of our school day is spent working on these books. Although it is deemed "history time," it's clear that there's quite a bit of subject overlap: reading historical non-fiction and biographies; writing outlines from the material; writing paragraphs and essays; typing or handwriting; spelling; designing comparison charts and fact sheets; searching for and choosing photos, posters or other art for each page; coloring or drawing original artwork; filling in maps; creating event timelines; sequencing page information and page design skills; and so on.

Obviously, as needed, we also dedicate school hours to developing our skills in these areas (for example, weekly quizzes on misspelled words, dedicated time for learning about *how* to draft an essay and *how* to do illustrations). But I love how **our history time is the practicum for so many other subjects.** We're able to streamline, reinforcing so many subjects and skills at once! This is a more natural and complete style of learning.

Setting Your Annual Teaching Goals

And what about you? Did you come up with some things you want to change about you, the teacher? Ah yes, it's always so much fun to look in the mirror!

Frankly, much of our teaching skills are developed on the job. And the "required" teaching skills vary from homeschool to homeschool because we are each teaching a unique set of students in a distinct location.

That's why **your goals need to be specifically tailored to your school and your situation**. You've done some self-evaluation and gotten feedback from your students. Now take that information, present it before the Lord, and pray, pray, pray for divine insight into how to best teach your kids. This process may take time. Listen for God to speak, and trust what he suggests you learn more about.

Next, work to get your questions answered. Talk to other homeschooling moms; read lots of books and blogs; and give yourself deadlines for completing these tasks.

Some changes require little research but instead require a new commitment. Are you pledging to start your school day at 8:00 a.m. instead of 10:00 a.m.? Do you desire to take the kids on a field trip once a month? Write down these commitments and even ask for accountability from your husband or another homeschooling mom, if need be.

Don't be afraid to make mistakes and to try something new and out of the box. Unsure about a new teaching style? Give it a try and see what happens! So much of my learning to be a teacher happens by trial and error. And boy, do I grow from year to year! Don't be afraid to dump what's not working and to embrace a new idea.

It's September... And I Still Don't Know What I'm Doing!

Even after you've done all this, you still may not have all the answers. **The school year may be about to start and you may find yourself more muddled and confused than before.** Been there, done that, got the ugly t-shirt. Here's what God has taught me in these times.

First of all, **don't worry**. No matter how much it looks like another homeschooling mom has it all together, I promise you that **she still has unanswered questions about how to do this homeschooling gig**. Here's the greatest homeschooling secret of all—none of us have all the answers! We will continue to discover and learn each year how to be better homeschooling moms. Just like parenting or marriage, there is no pinnacle that we will reach where we'll have it all figured out.

Second, **come to grips with the fact that homeschooling is HARD**. As a homeschool educator, there's a reason why you get comments like "Wow, I don't think I could ever do that!" I'm guessing that people who are, say, trash collectors, don't get those comments. I'm just saying (no offense to trash collectors, by the way).

Find comfort in the fact that you are doing one of the hardest jobs on the planet (not only being your kids' full-time *mom*, but their full-time *teacher*). This is a tough job that not every family has been called to, so be proud and carry this calling with confidence.

In the seasons when it seems there's a lot of hard manual labor in the homeschooling "fields," **ask God to show you some signs of the coming harvest**. You and I know the big-picture blessings of teaching our kids at home (otherwise we wouldn't have chosen this tough path). But in those moments when you need encouragement about why you're on this path, ask God to show you a glimpse of the beautiful fruit still growing underground.

Most of all, remember that God wants to help you! Be comforted by the fact that he's hand-picked *you* to teach *these children at this time*.

The Lord promises to walk with you and to tell you, moment by moment, how to specifically teach each child.

Action Plan:

1. Briefly list the subjects you're planning for each student, along with some quantifiable objectives for each.

2. How do you want to grow and change as a teacher? Do you want to implement a new teaching style? Make a honest list of your homeschooling struggles and seek out answers either from a trusted friend, by reading a book or following a blog (check out this book's "Additional Helpful Resources" section in the Appendix for ideas).

PART 2:

Develop A Schedule And A Curriculum Plan

(Editors note: There's a whole segment of homeschoolers who "unschool." You've probably met a few, or maybe you are one of them. These students don't have a set number of days and hours they're in school; they believe "life is the classroom." Study topics are mainly driven by the children's interests.

*Therefore, you might think the following chapters on schedules and curriculum plans are the antithesis of unschooling. **And if you're an unschooler, you might be tempted to skip them.** While I do agree that unschoolers will view these chapters through a different lens, **I still believe there's a lot here for those who eschew making rigid plans.***

*Hang in there with me, unschoolers. **Glean what you can from these chapters and apply the concepts to the limited schedules you do make.** Your moment is coming when we discover liberation from the schedule with limits in Chapters 9, 10, 11 and 12.)*

CHAPTER 5:

Create A Master School Year Calendar

Crafting a master school calendar is like putting together a very intricate puzzle. You know…one of those 1000 piece jobs with little color variation and line design. Overwhelming, taxing, and maddening.

Well, at least it can seem that way some years. Other years, it's like you're putting together one of those easy, 25-piece puzzles with your preschooler. Events line up, "puzzle piece placement" seems easy and obvious, and you find yourself done in no time.

While I can't guarantee that making a schedule each year will be like that super-easy princess puzzle you may have done last week with your four-year-old, I want to walk you through a **step-by-step process** to make it as easy as possible.

One quick aside before we get started: don't stress about the schedule-making process! **I'm sorry to tell you this, but life is going to happen and your perfectly-laid plans *will* get messed up.** We can't perfectly plan for an unforeseen future. We'll talk more about the delicate balance between planned schedules and real life interruptions in Chapter 10. **Yes, life may have interruptions, but we still need a structure and plan for the majority of our days** (which, thankfully, are usually average and fairly predictable). So let's press on and develop the best schedule we can using our known variables.

Setting Up Your Calendar

I choose to make my Master School Calendar on a Microsoft Excel Spreadsheet. Later on, I input key dates into a calendar program.

I like taking the additional step of writing everything in Excel first so I can view the entire year in one glance, then print the calendar as a one-page document. In addition, this extra step allows me to easily make adjustments and to quickly re-print out an updated master schedule for my desk.

I color code the weeks so as to quickly know when we are in school, when we are on a break, when holidays fall, when we have co-op days and the week number we're on for our specific curriculum.

However, **if it's easier for you to work solely in a calendar program, skip the Excel spreadsheet and enter the dates directly in a calendar program** such as My Well-Planned Day or Homeschool Tracker. This is what I eventually do after creating my helpful Excel spreadsheet.

Predetermined School Dates Or Your Own Schedule?

Are you going to register your school with the state under a larger charter organization or will you register as an independent school?

When you register with a charter school, you are required to follow their schedule. This means you will start school, end school and take school breaks on the dates they've outlined. This is a blessing for many homeschool families (yes! one less thing to figure out!) and makes laying the groundwork of your schedule (the outside pieces of your puzzle) fairly easy. If you've chosen the charter scenario, this step is simple: plug in the school dates into your Excel spreadsheet calendar and away you go.

If you've chosen to register your school independently, it's true you're going to have to sweat a little more at this step (more on the details in a few paragraphs). But for many families, crafting their own school schedule pays off in significant dividends throughout the year and is worth any extra sweat.

I have schooled both independently and under a charter school, and there are merits to both.

While I don't wish to get into a debate about independent versus charter here, I will say, however, that **if you want the ultimate freedom in your child's homeschool schedule and curriculum content, independent is the way to go.**

Living The Independent Life

Our family is currently registered as an independent school, and for us, there's no going back to "someone else's" school schedule. We really enjoy having a year-round schedule, taking a shorter summer break so that we can have **several mini-breaks throughout the year.**

Knowledge retention seems to go way up, and my frustration levels seem to go way down. Being on our own schedule also allows us to travel to relatives' houses and visit museums or landmarks when everyone else is *not*.

We finally made the switch to being an independent school when I learned that I was pregnant with our fourth child. The decision was further cemented when we learned a few months later that I would need a Caesarean and thus would have a longer recovery time — smack dab in the middle of January.

I reworked our schedule, starting our Christmas break a few days before the holiday and ending it in mid-February. While a six-week Christmas break seemed ridiculous at first, I realized that it was exactly what we needed as we welcomed a new baby into our fold. With this new schedule, I had time to recover and enjoy those precious first moments with our newborn, and the kids were able to make up the missed school days throughout the rest of the year.

There have been other times that we've enjoyed having complete control over our school schedule. We've enjoyed family vacations, a mission trip, art camps and other special times of learning — activities that would not have happened if we'd followed a typical school calendar. I also enjoy being able to adjust our schedule at the blink of an eye if we need to leave town to help with family, or if an unplanned ministry opportunity presents itself.

So, what are the additional steps needed to craft an independent school schedule?

First, determine the number of school days required by your state. This can typically be found on the state's department of education website, or via the Home School Legal Defense Association (HSLDA). My state, for example, requires a minimum of 175 school days.

Second, write in any holidays that you plan to celebrate. Maybe you take an annual trek to the zoo on December 14, for "International Monkey Day"? Or you're known as the family that hosts the "Bald and Free Holiday" Dinner Party on October 14? (No joke people, these are real holidays!). Seriously though, you know which holidays are important to your family and your homeschool. (Although we may just celebrate "Eight-Track Tape Day" on April 11 or "Public Sleeping Day" on February 28. I'm just saying.)

Third, write down any upcoming vacations, planned outings or other known upcoming life events. Are you planning a move? Are you pregnant or planning an adoption?

Fourth, are there any special museum exhibits or field trips you'd like to plan that are only during certain times of the year? For example, our neighboring town annually hosts a large Civil War re-enactment each year in March.

Fifth, write in any extra-curricular activities, including practice times, concerts, games, competitions, and the like. Perhaps your son has a music tournament next February in another state, and the following three months your daughter has speech tournaments every few weeks. Both require a lot of preparation and travel. Do you want to adjust the school schedule during those months so that they only have "school" three days a week so they can spend extra time practicing and preparing?

Lastly, decide how you want to structure your year overall. Do you want to school year-round with a break every 5 weeks or so? Do you want four-day school weeks? Or perhaps your husband has every Monday off so you choose to structure your school week from Tuesday to Saturday. Maybe you belong to a homeschooling co-op and you'd like to line up your schedule with their class days as much as possible. The possibilities are endless, so think about what would work best for your family. There are no rules except to make sure that you get in your required number of school days.

Action Plan:

1. Set up your master school calendar, either in Excel first or directly in a school planner or other calendar.

2. Determine if you'll be registering with a charter school (and thus be following their school schedule) or if you'll be an independent school (and thus need to create your own school schedule).

3. If registering as an independent school, plan your school dates accordingly, noting for holidays, vacations, upcoming events and other family activities.

CHAPTER 6:

Build A Curriculum Core For Each Student

*(Author's Note: **The activities described in Chapter 6, 7 and 8 are best completed simultaneously.** It's difficult to plan a detailed weekly homeschool schedule (Chapter 8) without first establishing a curriculum core (this chapter). At the same time, it's a challenge to determine a curriculum core without knowing what time you have available in the week (Chapter 8. And while these processes are happening, it's critical to consider your unique scheduling challenges (Chapter 7). I've split these topics into separate chapters just to keep the thought processes straight. But as we delve into these chapters, remember that you'll probably be doing all three at the same time.)*

We homeschoolers can be passionate and opinionated people.

Give us a platform we're zealous about, and we'll be *more than happy* to share our opinions to anyone who will listen.

This seems to be especially true when you ask us about curriculum and teaching styles.

We've all got our favorites, and *boy* we can't wait to tell you about them!

I have been on both sides of this conversation. I have been both the mom passionately telling another mom about the "ultimate" homeschool resource, and the mom who was just starting out, eagerly asking anyone she knew for advice on curriculum.

Seven years into my homeschooling journey, I am grateful to no longer be in either camp.

Not that I don't still recommend resources to other homeschoolers. And I am still constantly dialoging with other moms about curriculum ideas.

But here's the key change: I am no longer convinced that a certain curriculum or method is "the best." I have homeschooled long enough to see all kinds of resources working for all kinds of different families. **I have learned that no method, curriculum or style of learning is one-size-fits-all.**

Curriculum Choices: Following The Crowd?

Some homeschoolers are so loyal to a particular schooling philosophy that they greatly limit themselves when it comes to choosing curriculum. They only listen to "the right" voices in the homeschooling community. They only teach from a suggested group of pre-determined books. And they avoid resources from *those other publishers* like the plague.

If this is you, consider this your official wake-up call: *Stop the madness!* The world is filled with ways to teach kids. **None of them are perfect, but there are many, many good methods and resources out there**. No one's got the magic formula!

If you're pleased as punch with your math or science curriculum, seriously, keep rolling with it. But I can almost guarantee that it won't work for all of your kids, or that at some point this curriculum may not continue to work for *this* child.

It's just the way learning operates. Sometimes even when you figure out *how* a child is wired, it can still be difficult to find something that brings learning to life for them. And once you find a combination of effective resources, it may not work next year because our children are constantly growing and changing!

If we're going to rear not only smart kids but kids who fall in love with learning itself (which is the ultimate purpose of education), our teaching methods have to be rich, compelling and enticing.

I highly encourage you to come out of the limiting, constraining box that so many homeschoolers put themselves in. **Honestly take a look at what's available before you lock yourself (and your kids) into another year with the "right" curriculum if it does not truly serve the educational needs of your child.**

Take Time To Discover

Some curriculum choices are a slam dunk. You love it, the child loves it and you see their little minds grow and stretch.

Other subjects, however…well, they seem like that one cleverly crafted scavenger hunt clue that causes the most frustration and angst. Lots of thinking, searching and head-scratching going on here.

That's why you need to **give yourself lots of time when putting together your "Main Curriculum Core document"** each year. Solidify as many choices as possible, but realize that it may take time, effort and innovation before every box is filled.

I purposely am not giving my input here on "good" or "bad" curriculums because I don't know each of your children's educational needs. And like I said before, you may disagree with what I've deemed an "excellent choice" because it may or may not work for your family.

Go to the homeschool conventions and walk the floors — yes, *all* of the areas — **with an open mind**. See what's out there!

Get on the internet and read, read and read some more. Discover innovative ways that homeschooling families are building a love of learning in their kids.

Talk to your homeschooling friends and gather ideas and input. Do they (or did they) have kids with similar needs? If so, what works (or worked) for them?

Many of these ideas will be eclectic conglomerations of all sorts of methods and techniques. In fact, you'll probably find yourself becoming an eclectic educator as you begin making your own learning combinations. **The longer I homeschool the more varied my resources become!**

It's exciting when this happens because it means that we are not stuck in the rut of who our child was last year or even last month. **We are actively seeking to meet their changing learning needs**. This results in knowledge that is fresh and exciting to hungry and active minds.

Chapter 11 details more about creating this type of "living" curriculum. In the meantime, let's begin the process of outlining curriculum choices by creating a place to write down the curriculum names and ideas.

Create Your "Main Curriculum Core" Template

Here's how to build a simple document to hold your main curriculum choices for each child.

Open a new Excel document.

In the top row, type "(Your Child's Name) (School Year) Curriculum Core." Merge and center the box to fill four columns across the top.

In the next row, type "Subject," "Curriculum," "Topics," **"Frequency," "Teaching Time Needs" and "Shared."**

You've now created a basic schedule template! Before you go any further, **save the document** so that you have a template to use from year to year.

Now, create a new sheet *within the master document* **for each child.** This way you can easily switch between sheets to see each child's curricula list.

To create a new sheet in the document, **click on a tab at the bottom of the document to create a new sheet** (it may say "Sheet 1"). A new sheet should appear. Copy the information from your previous sheet and paste it to this new sheet (make any necessary adjustments to the height and width of the columns and rows). Type in the new child's name in the top row of the sheet.

Repeat this process so that each child has his own sheet.

Click "Save As" and rename your document, entering this school year's dates in the title.

Fill In The Template

Now it's time to fill in the template with this year's basic curriculum information. Repeat this process for each child's curriculum sheet.

"Subject." List the subjects that this child will cover this year. To give a comprehensive scope of what the child will be learning, **include subjects taught at a co-op and other extracurricular activities** such as art classes, music lessons and sports.

"Curriculum." List here the **main books and resources** you'll use to teach each particular subject. Are you using the curriculum exactly as it's planned, or are you making some modifications?

If you're gathering together various resources to make your own or making major modifications, consider creating a separate document to detail this information (more on this in Chapter 11).

"Topics." Although this document's goal is simply to hold a child's master curriculum list, **you may choose to add more subject detail** (such as "Addition, Subtraction" or "Marine Animals"). This additional information can be included in the "Topics" column.

If you wish to further flesh out a topic (by adding either additional resources or subtopics), **create an additional document with more detail** (more on that in Chapter 8).

"Frequency." This is the **number of times per week** (or the days of the week, if you know this) that the student will work on this subject. How do you determine how much weekly class time to give each subject? You could base this on what the curriculum recommends, but ultimately, this is up to what you deem necessary.

"Shared?" This column's information states if the subject and/or curriculum will be shared with another student. This helps in determining how much teaching time (and preparation time) may be needed overall.

"Teaching Time Needs." Will the student work independently on this curriculum, or will it require a lot of hands-on-teaching? Can you teach several students at once? Does the curriculum require a lot of preparation? This column helps you track this type of information so you can see at-a-glance how much overall time you'll need to make this curriculum list a reality.

Take A Second Look

Now that you have all the information about the curricula in one location, re-examine your choices using the following questions:

- Have you covered all the necessary subjects?

- Can any of the subjects be combined?

- Does the curriculum still seem to be a good fit for each student's needs?

- If you detailed a curriculum into topics, does the number of topics seem an adequate amount to teach this year?

- Do you need to create additional document(s) to further detail a particular subject?

- Do you need to adjust the number of times per week your child will learn a specific subject?

- Does the overall workload seem adequate for your student's age, grade level and maturity?

- Is the amount of independent work appropriate for your student's current study skills and habits?

- Are the demands on your time (whether for pre-class preparation or in-class teaching) realistic?

Action Plan:

1. Carefully consider your curriculum choices for next year. After honestly reviewing all of your options, do you feel like the curriculum you've chosen is the best choice for your family's current situation? Will these choices help you meet your ultimate homeschooling goals?

2. Follow the steps above to create your "Main Curriculum Core" template.

3. Fill in the details about your curriculum choices in the document.

4. After looking at the subjects side-by-side, are these curriculum choices still the best for your family?

CHAPTER 7:

Consider Your Unique Learning Environment

One of the greatest challenges of homeschooling is that your children are continually growing and changing—and so is your homeschooling environment! Some of these changes can be anticipated. Others are completely unexpected and out of your control.

However, there are challenges that remain from year to year (though the details may change). How do you schedule each of your three kids' school subjects and extracurricular activities? What about your child's sport schedule (which this year is soccer)? And let's not forget the everyday challenges all homeschoolers face: cooking, cleaning, laundry, grocery shopping, meal planning, ministry or job commitments… the list goes on!

Homeschooling doesn't exist in a vacuum—it revolves around real life! Therefore, all the planning in the world is meaningless if it isn't developed within the daily reality of life situations like these. If not considered in the overall plan, each of these scenarios can throw a major curveball into a perfectly planned homeschool schedule. That's why, before we begin labeling and dedicating time to each subject (Chapter 8), **we're going to identify scheduling challenges and discuss scheduling strategies to encourage smooth and easy learning.**

Examine Scheduling Challenges

Let's talk about *real* homeschool life for a moment, shall we?

Squirmy kids who can't sit still for more than 5 minutes. Babies and toddlers who need extra attention. Younger students who need mom's full attention for nearly all their assignments. One-on-one, complex instruction for older students in advanced subjects. Students that zone out in the afternoons. (Enter your homeschooling challenges here).

To top it all off, each of these kids are on their own unique learning schedule — with their own curriculum lists and extracurricular activities!

(Deep breaths... deep breaths...). Come on, hang in there with me.

Situations like these are the mainstays of homeschool life (although that doesn't make them any easier!). Every homeschool has distinct challenges — some more than others. This is what makes your learning environment unique from mine.

Regardless, these situations can throw a major wrench in your homeschool day if you're not prepared. While it's impossible to identify and discuss every possible challenge, let's look at those listed above.

Challenge # 1: Each Child's Schedule Is Different

While this challenge is listed last in the text above, this is the foundational challenge that we must all address if we have multiple children.

Consider this hypothetical example: This year, Todd's tenth grade subjects include Science, History, Writing, Philosophy, Grammar, Math, Speech/Debate, and Literature (plus violin lessons). Betsy's sixth grade subject list also includes Science, History, Math and Writing (which she will do at the same time as Todd), but she also has Spanish, Cursive Writing, Spelling and an outside Art class. And then there's six-year-old Cayden. He has Phonics, Handwriting, Spelling, Math, History, Science and Karate twice a week.

If you have more than one child, clearly you need a schedule for each.

In Chapter 3, we discussed outlining unique goals for the year for each child. While there's hopefully some subject overlap (the benefits of this are also discussed in Chapter 3), **each child is going to be following his own learning trajectory.**

In addition, **consider making a schedule for any non-school aged children** as well. While baby Jillian may not be a student yet, her life does follow a pattern that interacts with how the rest of your school day happens (we'll talk more about that below in "Challenge #3: Babies and Toddlers).

Challenge #2: Squirmy Kids

Granted, this seems to mainly strike those with younger kids, but some of us have older children with attention disorders that are also plagued with the squirmies. Some kids are just kinesthetic learners and need to move around a lot.

Here's how I've handled it in our school. When considering how to arrange the order of a "squirmy" child's school day, I try **to alternate between independent, solitary activities (writing, independent reading and bookwork) and physical, social activities (an interactive class game, one-on-one time with a sibling, free play in the backyard).**

For example, I wouldn't ask this type of learner to read for thirty minutes and then to independently work on math for thirty minutes because I know I'd find him incredibly distracted and unfocused. Instead, I'd break up these two solitary activities with a social or kinesthetic activity—perhaps a planned all-class teaching time, or a chance to run on the treadmill or ride bikes outside. This child needs lots of scheduled breaks, especially after he's been asked to sit down for a while. I'd also try to **break the child's day into smaller chunks,** switching topics every thirty minutes or so (or switching even more frequently if the child is both younger and naturally squirmy).

Challenge #3: Babies and Toddlers

When it comes to homeschooling with a baby in the house, one blessing is that most babies take a least one nap a day. I try to arrange our schedule so that we get as much done as possible during the baby's nap time. In fact, I will specifically plan those subjects that require my one-on-one coaching during the younger one's nap times.

But, oh, the dreaded days when babies grow into toddlers and then preschoolers, all the while slowing outgrowing their need for naps! Don't get me wrong—this is a precious childhood age and a wonderful parenting time to savor. It's just not the easiest stage when you're also trying to homeschool.

When naptime is no longer a viable option for taking care of the "meatier" parts of a homeschool day, I employ two other strategies.

The first is to **schedule time for older siblings to play with the toddler or preschooler.** Not only is the younger child thrilled to have a dedicated playmate, **the older child is learning responsibility, humility, and an others-focused attitude.** In addition, priceless bonds are being built between the children (which may be one of your main reasons for homeschooling in the first place). Present this time as a wonderful reward for the older child (now they are old enough to be a helper with the younger kids!) and remind him that this is an extra "break" in his school studies. Set aside a special box of toys and games only to be used for this time together.

And what about those times when a little one isn't napping or playing with another child? I designate a corner of our school area for this little one and **give him some special, age-appropriate activities that only come out during school time.** These activities, which some call "busy bags," are simple household objects gathered to make several sorting, coloring and stacking-type games. Oodles of ideas abound on the internet, and you're welcome to follow my "Homeschooling: Toddler Learning and Busy Activities" Pinterest board for added inspiration. Along with teaching a young child important skills like focusing, listening and paying attention, some busy bag activities encourage early literacy and number skills. This time of independent quiet play is also important for a child's social development because

75

the child learns at an early age not to expect to always be entertained by others.

Challenge #4: Students That Need Lots Of One-On-One Teaching

There could be several reasons for this: the student may be very young and not literate yet (and therefore can't read his own assignments); the student may be older and needs adult perspective and interaction with a difficult subject; a student of any age may find a subject challenging and therefore requires additional teacher instruction time; or the curriculum may require lots of active teaching time.

The bottom line is that you can't be in two places at once! If you know in advance that you'll have one or two children that fall into the above categories, **consider ways to arrange your teaching time** so that you are available to help when needed. Don't schedule your daughter's high-need-teaching subject in the same time-slot as your five-year-old son who is unable to read. **Examine one student's schedule against another and create the best possible arrangement**. More on that in a few pages.

Challenge #5: Natural Biorhythms

Like any other human, your students probably have segments of their day when their minds are fresh and active, and other segments when they're simply ready to shut down for a while. Call it our body's natural biorhythms, the two o'clock doldrums, or simply the inability for students to focus late in the day. Regardless, we have to be proactive in planning around these natural ebbs and flows.

First, watch how a student's dietary intake affects his ability to learn. If a child eats sugary cereals (or a breakfast without a lot of protein or complex carbohydrates), no wonder he gets that deer-in-the-headlights look around 10 a.m.! A drop in blood sugar often results in fatigue and a reduced attention span. Consider what your child eats and when he eats it. Reformulating breakfast, adding a morning snack or changing up lunch could make a huge difference in a child's attention span. Also, did you know that drinking water wakes up your brain and prepares you to learn? Experiment and see what works best for your child.

But even with a perfectly balanced diet, there probably still will be times of the day when learning comes more easily than others. Recognize this upfront when doing your planning and make adjustments. For example, if math is really hard for your daughter, don't schedule it in the afternoon when she is typically a little cranky and ready for a break from school. Instead, schedule her math first thing in the morning, or whenever you notice her mind is freshest.

Challenge #6: Scheduled Activities Outside The Home

You may have regular, planned activities such as sports, music lessons or outside classes with other homeschoolers. Maybe you have a Mom's Group that you lead every Wednesday morning, or a part-time job may be part of your weekly routine. Regardless of the situation, school may be limited on these days and heavy on others.

Determine in advance when you need to block off time for these activities.

For example, when I was pregnant with my fourth baby, my prenatal visits were on Fridays, so I left a few hours in the morning open on Friday. **I knew this in advance, and I planned for it.**

Challenge #7: Unscheduled Activities (AKA Real Life)

This is a challenge that we all share! Kids get sick. A friend may need your help at the last minute. It's just the way life works.

Leave a section of your schedule open for doctor's appointments, quick errands, or other activities that may come up unexpectedly. Plan a few "free times" in your week so that when unplanned events come up, you can take care of these then (we'll talk more about dealing with life's unexpected curves in Chapter 10).

This planned margin in your week is critical. It can make the difference between a schedule that works and one that doesn't.

Schedule two to three hours of "open time" on Wednesday afternoon (or whatever day and time works for you). This doesn't mean that you are hoping that these unexpected life occurrences happen between one and three o'clock on a Wednesday afternoon! You're simply making space at this time, knowing, that if there are interruptions at another time during the week, this can be your catch-up time. **And if you have a relatively uneventful week (you know… it could happen) spend this time catching up on other subjects or just relaxing and having fun.**

Challenge # 8: What, You Have A House To Run Too?

Ah, yes… if only we could homeschool without the added "home" responsibilities. Those darn dishes just keep piling up while we're happily doing science experiments and creating salt dough relief maps. The best advice? **Develop systems for all of the household tasks and make them a part of your schedule.**

And by all means, engage your kids in these activities (consider this their "real world lesson" for the day)! One homeschooling mom I know says, **"If I can teach them at least to do their own laundry and to cook their own food, I'll know that they can survive on their own."**

While kids can be trained to be excellent helpers around the home, ladies, there's no shame in hiring a housekeeper (if you are financially able) to regularly handle those deep cleaning tasks. And even if a housekeeper comes on a regular basis, there still will be *plenty* of household maintenance practice for your kids (dishes, cooking, picking up, laundry).

"Additional Helpful Resources" in the Appendix has a list of my favorite websites and books to help with meal planning, once a month grocery shopping, and chores.

Keep On Trucking

If your homeschool contains any (or all) of these scenarios and you don't know how you'll solve these scheduling challenges yet, do

not fret! I include this section *before* we plug in the times/days of each subject so that you can "wear" these challenges as "lenses" while you're making scheduling decisions.

These are complicated issues that take time and creativity to solve! **Don't let these issues bog down your schedule planning. Keep moving!** Just **keep these challenges in the back of your mind** while you move on to the next step: building the schedule itself.

Action Plan:

1. Think through your school's unique challenges. What strategies would be helpful in streamlining your schedule?

2. Do you need to do additional research to get workable solutions to these issues? Talk to other moms, take a look at the additional resources here and find answers.

CHAPTER 8:

Draft A Weekly Schedule

If stopwatches, to-do lists and hour-by-hour schedules make you quiver with excitement (yes, I'm talking to you, Type-A moms), this is the chapter you've been waiting for!

This is the chapter where our school goals and plans transform from mere ideas and theories to specified days and times in a school week. It's when we decide that we will do Writing on Tuesdays and Thursdays at 11:00 a.m. and Math every morning at 9:30 a.m.

However, if scheduled timeslots and frequencies for school subjects make you break out into a cold sweat, then take a deep breath and repeat after me: *My schedule is only a piece of paper. My schedule works for me, and I am not a slave to it.* Again, this tension of living with (but not under) a schedule will be discussed in more detail in the following chapter, so hang in there.

If it makes you feel better, the schedule you create here can be as detailed (or as simple) as you'd like. You are in control here.

Ready to jump in?

How To Set Up A Schedule

Give each child their own schedule, and then arrange all the schedules together in one document. I use Microsoft Excel for this preliminary schedule planning stage.

Open a new Excel document.

In the farthest left column, begin typing in time slots for the school day (leave the top corner box, "A:1," blank so that everything lines up correctly). The time slots should run down the left side of your document.

Divide the time slots into half-hour increments: 8:00-8:30 a.m., 8:30-9:00 a.m., 9:00-9:30 a.m. and so on.

Make as many half-hour time increments as you deem necessary. I include time slots that start before and after our school day so as to include time for morning chores, evening chores and extra-curricular activities. Since the "home" and "school" times are inordinately mixed for homeschoolers, it's easier to make a master schedule that includes all of the child's general objectives for a given day (more on that in a few paragraphs).

In the top row of the document, begin typing in the days of the week. The days (Monday, Tuesday, Wednesday, etc.) should run across the top of your document, each in its own column. Again, leave the top corner box "A:1" blank.

The locations where your day row and time column intersect are your specific time slots for each day.

Highlight all of the boxes and turn on all box borders to more clearly see divisions between time and subjects.

Insert another row at the top. Merge and center all of the columns of the top row. Type in "(child's name) Schedule". Highlight the text and turn it white. Highlight the boxes of the top row and fill the color in black. **Now your schedule has a title.**

Enter your schedule anchors. This would be "lunch," "snack break," "chores," or the things that everyone does together.

You've now created a basic schedule template! Before you go any further, **save the document** so that you have a template to use from year to year.

Now, let's create a new sheet *within the master document* **for each child.** This way you can easily switch between sheets to see each child's schedule.

To create a new sheet in the document, **click on a tab at the bottom of the document to create a new sheet** (it may say "Sheet 1"). A new sheet should appear. Copy the information from your previous sheet and paste it to this new sheet (make any necessary adjustments to the height and width of the columns and rows). Type in the new child's name in the top row of the sheet.

Repeat this process so that each child has his own sheet.

Click "Save As" and rename your document, entering this school year's dates in the title.

Plug Subjects And Activities Into Specified Times

This is a **messy, complicated stage** that takes lots of arranging to make all the pieces fit!

Don't say you weren't warned.

But truly, once you've established **this backbone to your homeschool week**, your days will be far smoother and you will get so much more accomplished!

If things get especially hairy and complicated while you are planning (and your eyes are starting to cross!), print out each child's schedule and lay the schedules side-by-side to compare what each student is doing at a given moment of the day. If adjustments need to be made, it's easy to make the changes in the Excel document and print it out again.

Give yourself freedom to make mistakes. You won't nail the exact schedule times for each subject the first time you try it! Just start moving through the process and edit as you go. Take as long as you need to get all the pieces to line up.

You won't always follow this schedule perfectly, and some days you will abandon it completely (whether by choice or one of life's little curveballs). However, **this weekly schedule is your place to go** when you feel like you've drifted off the beaten path and things feel off kilter.

For those of you who feel **confined and stifled by a schedule** (and those homeschoolers who've realized that real learning often happens *outside* the schedule), rest assured that Chapters 9, 10, 11 and 12 cover this topic in depth. So for now, **let's create a solid framework**—a direction and purpose for our day. Later on **we'll talk about finding freedom within its boundaries.** Deal?

Step 1: Schedule Timeslots for Daily Anchors

Give the schedule daily "anchors": fixed points in the day that everyone does together, no matter what the day holds. Examples of this would be "snack break," "lunch" or "afternoon rest time." Determine the time of day, and then type this information into the appropriate time slot of each day. For example, type "lunch" at noon for Monday through Friday if that's when you'd always like to have lunch.

Include **chores and other all-family activities as schedule anchors** too. As stay-at-home moms, we still have children who need to eat, clothes that need to be washed, bathrooms that need to be cleaned— you name it!—in the midst of our homeschooling activities. And as children age, they can help out with these household basics. Since this is not just a homeschooling schedule but a master daily schedule for the child, establish anchors in the day such as "morning chores" and "evening chores" so that kids can accomplish these goals too.

There are entire books with methods and systems for accomplishing these key homemaking tasks. A few are mentioned in this chapter's resource section. The bottom line is simple: Pick a system and make these designated times as "anchors" for your school day.

In addition, I highly recommend you **include open, free times in your schedule** to accomplish those unscheduled, last minute activities that come up. We covered this in more detail in Chapter 7.

Step 2: Schedule Shared Subjects

Open (and print, if necessary) the document you created in Chapter 5 that lists each child's subjects, the subjects' weekly frequency and the corresponding curricula. Your goal is to input each of these subjects into a specific time slot on the individual schedules.

Next, identify the shared subjects that can be taught together. Again, this is where it's beneficial to have students studying as many similar concepts as possible (for example, everyone is studying 1850-1950 as this year's history topic). For more information about how to teach shared subjects, re-read "Suggestions for Setting Objectives" in Chapter 4.

Designate a day/time for these shared subjects and enter them into each child's schedule. For example, under the 11:00 time slot, enter "History" for Monday, Tuesday, Wednesday, Thursday and Friday for each student.

Step 3: Schedule Subjects With Lots Of Hands-On Teaching

Next, looking at all of the students' subjects as a whole, **consider the ones that require the most of your attention and the least of your attention** (whether due to the curriculum style or the student's individual needs). For example, your Kindergartner's Handwriting time requires all of your hands-on attention (because you need to watch him form his letters), while your eighth grader's Literature time may require little to no hands-on teaching time (because he's simply reading the novels and completing the required essays as dictated in the curriculum). **If your students have subjects that require a lot of your hands-on teaching time, try to schedule these subjects at the same time as another student that has a subject that requires very little of your time.**

That's great, but what if you have a lot more subjects that require your one-on-one attention than subjects with little to no teaching time? Think about these options.

First, consider a different curriculum for that subject. This can be a heartbreaking decision, especially if you adore a specific curriculum! However there are many, many ways to teach a concept. Cathy Duffy's 101 Top Picks for Homeschool Curriculum is a great resource for identifying quality curriculum. Her book is especially helpful because it identifies the curriculum's required amount of active teaching time, along with the curriculum's teaching style.

Sometimes, however, there's just no substitute for a particular curriculum (that's how I feel about my writing, history and math curricula). Therefore, perhaps another subject's curriculum (that you aren't as attached to) can be switched out? If so, this too can free up your teaching time.

If you still need more time, build additional activities into a school-aged child's day that won't require your complete attention. This may require a little creative thinking and schedule juggling!

Last year, I planned a lot of subjects that required my hands-on teaching. When I started schedule planning it became immediately evident that I needed to find several time slots in the week for these one-on-one teaching times while the other children were occupied elsewhere. The kids had just taken up running, and I'd also desired that the kids deepen their relationships with each other. So, I instituted two new "subjects" in the kids' schedule: "Treadmill Time" and "Sibling Bonding Time". While **one of the children was running on the treadmill (a major treat in our home!) another was playing with a sibling**. That left the fourth child's schedule open for me to have one-on-one teaching time. Later on in the week, the kids switched roles and there was another open teaching time for me. Necessity truly is the mother of invention!

Lastly, if you just can't fit it in, consider skipping the subject this year or combining it with another subject. Yes, you heard me right—**I am giving you permission to skip or consolidate subjects.** Obviously this should only be done for a season, if done at all. It is not a first-line defense.

But even if you aren't "scheduling" time for a certain subject (like Spelling, for example), I challenge you to not teach your child about it this year! We pass on so much information to our kids in their everyday learning that it virtually impossible for them not to grow in knowledge if we are providing them with a solid, well-rounded education (my unschooling friends have taught me this). Of course, everyone has a different definition of a "solid, well-rounded education," but I think you know what I'm saying: don't skimp on the basics (for us that's Bible, Math, History, Reading, Writing and Science) and the rest will naturally flow.

By all means, challenge your students and teach them as much as possible! Just do the best you can with the time you've been given. If teaching 10 different subjects to four different kids will make you a stressed out teacher (let alone wife and mom!) **it's better to consolidate, simplify and pare down than to jeopardize the precious relationships you're building with your family.** If they don't pick it up now, I guarantee they will pick it up later if they really need it.

Step 3: Schedule Additional Subjects

Add any additional subjects to the children's schedules that you may have missed.

Make adjustments to the schedules as necessary.

Yep, this step is pretty straightforward.

Step 4: Add More Schedule Detail (If You Want)

Daily general objectives for a subject. Although you may be teaching History at 11:00 a.m. every day for all students, it may help to list a rough outline of what information you'll be teaching each day. For example, in Monday's history slot, you might also write "introduce topic, core reading and narration." If this concept helps you, include it. If this complicates your schedule and causes you frustration, don't worry about it!

Use color and capital letters. To visually break up the schedule, **consider color coding time slots by type**. In my document, dark gray is "school time"; medium gray is "chores/extracurricular activities"; no tint is "meals," "breaks," or "rest time." You can also **use all capital letters for anchor points** in the day like "lunch," or "snack break."

Include an alternate day. If you have an activity that happens every other week or once a month, think about adding an alternate schedule for that day. For example, every other Friday our family meets for a Science lab and play date with another homeschooling family. On these Fridays, we spend only a brief time doing other subjects. Therefore, I have an alternate schedule for these Science Lab Fridays.

Now What Do I Do With This?

Give a copy to your kids for their reference. Tell them that this schedule is a general guide for how the days can run. This gives kids, especially those who have a hard time sitting still, confidence in knowing the start and end times of a typical school day. In the same way that we like to know that our work day will end at a certain time, most kids enjoy having a basic outline of their school day.

Transfer the information to a homeschool planner software. This may seem like an extra step. However by entering in this information into a print or online program such as those by Homeschool Tracker, the software will automatically use the schedule to track attendance.

Place a copy at your desk (or another safe place) for quick reference. Again, this is a great guide for those days when you aren't sure where to start. It's also a great comfort on days when you feel overwhelmed because you realize, yes, you *will* cover everything you need to in your schedule—eventually.

Action Plan:

1. Build your Weekly Schedule Template in Excel. Create separate sheets inside the main document for each student.

2. Plug each subject into your chosen times for each day. Consider how each student's scheduled subject times interacts with the others, and make changes as necessary.

3. Be patient with the process, altering as needed until you're happy with the final product.

4. Print out several copies. Place them at your desk and give them to the students. Consider inputting the information into a homeschooling planning software.

PART 3:

...And Get Ready to Be Flexible

CHAPTER 9:

The Fine Art Of Living Within
(But Not Under) A Schedule

One of the greatest comforts to me when I first started homeschooling was my daily checklist.

That first year I purchased a box curriculum, gathered the necessary school supplies and organized all our books and workbooks on our school shelf. I printed out our schedule that outlined all that we were to accomplish each day, including the (what I deemed *very lovely)* box to check when the assignment was completed. *Learning could now begin,* I proudly thought to myself, sighing contentedly.

And boy, did it ever begin. Except the real student wasn't my kid—it was me.

My On-The-Job Training

My first student—an adorable, high-energy little boy of four—was to be my first teacher.

Back then, this inquisitive little one loved exploring! Stacking! Sorting! Being read to! *So why didn't he love this super-fabulous curriculum like I'd been promised,* I wondered. Why the fights when we sat down and "did school," even school that was supposed to be "good for preschoolers"?

Fast forward two years. Our second son was now old enough to "start" preschool (no, I hadn't learned yet that kids really start their education the day they're born. And I *really* hadn't bought into the concept yet that, as a rule, most little boys aren't ready for formal education until they're at least five or six). I now had a four-year-old and a six-year old, and dog-gone-it, they were *going* to learn! I pushed and pushed, making them sit down to write letters and to do simple math worksheets.

But oh, the drama. All they wanted to do was run outside, look for bugs and play with their toy cars! "Come on…why can't you get this?!" I said one day to them, exasperated that once again our scheduled half-hour of math had resulted in only a few completed math problems.

And let's not forget the times they were sick and we spent our "school time" in a doctor's office because of a sore throat or ear infection. Or, heaven forbid, there were even times we had to ditch the schedule because we needed to buy groceries or run to the bank! I became annoyed at these life occurrences because, once again, my perfectly planned day had been upset.

Ironically, I couldn't see that real learning *was occurring*—outside of my forced homeschool schedule. The boys could tell me all about different kinds of cars. They built intricate forts out of pillows and blankets and were experts at playing knights. My oldest could name and identify nearly two dozen flowers (something he'd taught himself by simply asking "Mommy, what type of flower is that?" on our daily walks).

But, hard-headed, narrow-minded educator that I was, all I saw was that what I'd been trying to teach them wasn't sticking. **I only noticed that my boxes were *not* getting checked each day, and that we were falling farther and farther behind our homeschool schedule.**

As these "disruptions" became more frequent, I began ditching schoolbooks or not completing them at all because we'd run out of time during the day. Immense guilt piled up as a little voice inside me taunted, "Why did you think you could ever do this?" Sometimes this voice—one that I noticed also drove me to perfectionism and to set unrealistic expectations for myself—said, "They just need to be pushed harder." I was convinced that they were the problem; that *they* just needed to obey and adapt to our "correct" schedule.

People would comment on how smart and inquisitive my boys were. "You must be doing something right!" they'd say. I would simply smile and think, *Oh, if you only knew what our homeschool days were like.* I received their intended compliments as another chance to beat myself up because I felt like I was living duplicitously. "You're not really teaching your kids," I would hear inside. "If they only knew how much you *weren't* getting done in the day."

I'm sorry to say that things continued on this way for a long time. I switched our schedule around. I changed curriculums. I read and read about other teaching methods. The kids did respond somewhat favorably to changes I made, but there were still many days of tension and difficulty. **That frustration—the tension of *not* getting it all done—remained and clouded my confidence as an educator.**

I held on to my rigid schedule because I took my teaching responsibility seriously! I needed proof and reassurance that, yes, I was indeed giving them a rigorous, grade-appropriate education.

It finally all collided that afternoon at the coffee shop. I was disillusioned and bitter, and my poor kids were probably just as exhausted as I was from "school."

After that incident, God gave me a reprieve from teaching. He allowed me to stand back and draft the goals you read about in Chapter 1. Forget the stupid schedule—was this homeschooling gig ultimately working? Was real learning happening? Were relationships being strengthened? It took some time (and God had to work on my stubborn heart) but finally, **box-checking no longer became my pass/fail indicator of accomplishment.**

Living without any sort of a schedule seemed ludicrous, however. An archer needs a target before he shoots his arrows, even if that target is moving. Otherwise, why waste the arrow? I had given up my career and all of my free time to teach these kids. You bet your bottom dollar I was going to be purposeful and not waste the time!

Eventually through prayer, tears and slowly releasing my grip of control, I learned to let God fill our days with both planned and spontaneous learning. Thankfully, **God taught me how to live within the confines of a schedule without being a slave to it.**

A Guidepost Not A Prison

Walk with me here as I share **this beautiful tension of living "in but not under" a homeschooling schedule.**

First, your schedule is still an extremely powerful guidepost for day-to-day schooling. Your schedule is your reference book, your manual. It's where you go when you begin thinking about how a typical school day or week will play out. However, this schedule is not written in stone.

If you've been homeschooling for two minutes you can probably guess why.

Sometimes kids don't understand an assignment and your class time is simply spent explaining (and not doing the schoolwork). Some days the kids get it right away, but want to goof off instead of working. Other times the work is self-explanatory and the learning time goes much quicker than expected.

And sometimes students really dig into a specific subject and a beautiful flow of learning occurs. When this happens, my suggestion is, if at all possible, forget the time parameters you've established and let your kids ride the wave of learning exploration.

Room To Explore

Some of my favorite homeschool days are when we start reading or searching on the internet about a certain topic, and then end up happily exploring so much more than I'd planned. To me, this is real learning! The kids are asking questions, you're digging for answers, and that information leads to even more exploration. **It also demonstrates to me that they love what we're learning (and when you love something, don't you tend to remember it?).**

Case in point: A few months back we were studying World War II. You know, happy topics like concentration camps, Pearl Harbor, atomic bombs, horrific battles...and of course, the story of three power-hungry dictators and their quest to take over the world. On this particular day, we were studying Hitler, his propaganda and why it was so effective on the German populace.

Naturally, we ran across several posters depicting the glory of "Die Fuhrer" (Hitler). But there was **one poster that was particularly offensive to my kids.** It depicted a glorified, triumphant Hitler holding a Nazi flag with a sea of soldiers behind him. What made the poster over-the-top, even downright blasphemous, was that there was a dove (surrounded by beams of light) that looked like it was about to descend upon Hitler's head! **My kids made the connection instantly**: "Mom, that's a dove! That's like when Jesus was anointed by the Holy Spirit during His baptism! What are the Nazis saying—that Hitler is a savior like Christ? What?!" So we talked about how, yes, over time the German people became convinced that he was their savior, following him in a cult-like frenzy.

We found some of Hitler's quotes, one of them being, "I have not come into the world to make men better, but to make use of their weaknesses." We were all shocked at the contrast—the downright mockery!—Hitler was making of Jesus' statement in John 12:46: "I have come as a light to shine in this dark world, so that all who put their trust in me will no longer remain in the dark." We pulled out our Bibles and began looking up scripture after scripture that detailed Jesus' beautiful servant heart—clearly a contrast to Hitler and his actions.

"How could the German people follow a man with such an evil purpose?" the kids wanted to know. I explained how they had been swayed by the Nazis' smooth speeches. This propaganda, along with a strong desire for national pride, forced the Germans to check their logic at the door. "It was a slow progression," I said. Then we discussed the importance of knowing God's word and of using it as the filter of truth.

Armed with this information, **the kids wanted to create a comparison chart** between Hitler and Jesus (which they titled "Who Is The True King?"). **It was one of those beautiful spur-of-the-moment assignments that exploratory learning affords.** They were excited by the project, and I was thrilled with the learning connections they'd made.

Did our discussion extend beyond the half-hour I'd scheduled? Yep. That day "History" was more like an hour and a half. **But look at what else we covered**: Bible (specifically Christ's character). Bible Study Skills (practice in looking up scriptures). Art (they looked at Nazi propaganda posters and paintings of Christ). Logic (creating a comparison chart).

I didn't want to jeopardize the natural flow and excitement of learning so that we could stick to our schedule. That day, we didn't get to Spelling and Grammar. I didn't have time to do my one-on-one

Phonics/Reading time with my kindergartner. But obviously we covered other important topics, and **my kids were lost in a love for learning**. That is priceless (and frankly, one of my big-picture homeschooling goals)!

A month after the "Hitler learning time," I witnessed the **lasting effects of exploratory learning.**

Our family was gathered to celebrate Mother's Day. My boys were asking their great-grandfather about his World War II experiences, which lead to an entire family discussion. When the topic of Hitler came up, I (tried to) share a few of the Hitler quotes we'd read. I know I flubbed the exact words because **my eight-year-old, who had been engaged and astutely participating in the conversation, quickly corrected my quote recitation**! Alright, I was annoyed that my kid had showed me up, but I was also proud that he knew the info so well that *he could correct me*!

Long-term learning had happened here, even though we stretched our schedule that day to make it happen.

Holding The Line... Or Letting Go?

When do you keep the teaching on schedule, and when do you say *sayonara* to the structure? I'm going to leave that answer to Mark Twain's famous quote: "I never let my school get in the way of my education."

If you see natural learning happening, go for it! Obviously we can't abandon the schedule structure every day (then there would be no such thing as a schedule), but if you see natural learning happening, I'd encourage you to let go of your timetables.

I share this because we homeschoolers can get **downright obsessed with having a specific time and a specific curriculum for each subject.** It's much easier to think of our History time as a certain time of the day, and our Writing time as another, with specific "lessons" for each (after all, that's how the schools do it). While this is helpful in determining a schedule (and an outline for what, when and how to teach a subject), sometimes it's not a reflection of how learning actually occurs.

Some homeschoolers argue, yes, we do need to stay on topic without branching off into other subjects in a given teaching time. They'd say, "No, this is History time. We're only talking about the Renaissance today, not its art. We'll cover Art and Art History on Wednesday from 1:00 to 2:00." I can understand this teaching style. Some topics are so big that, in order to cover everything, it's important to keep a structure, a flow (and a time) for learning each aspect of it.

But for those teachers who've taken a more free-flowing approach to learning, I wanted to demonstrate that **it is possible (and I'd argue necessary) to have some sort of schedule amidst exploratory learning**. It may not rigidly follow what you've outlined, but it's a backbone and structure to the learning time.

105

Planned Subject Overlap

There have been seasons in our schooling when I've completely blurred the lines between subjects and, thus, deliberately ignored the schedule's parameters. Why? Simply put, **there are so many ways to gather and express knowledge that, in order to keep learning exciting and new, I combine subjects**.

Historical and scientific topics often lend themselves to this type of combined subject learning. Instead of separate learning times, I combine the times I'd allocated for each subject and just let them all happen together.

When we studied the 1920s, the kids each created a large, foldable "newspaper." Follow along as we document **all the subjects covered in this one project:**

- **History**: Learned about key historical events and people

- **Science:** Discovered key technological advances

- **Fashion Design, Music Appreciation, Cinematography:** Examined music, fashion, lifestyle and entertainment

- **Outlining and Essay Writing:** Wrote essays about events, people and technology

- **Internet and Book Research, Photography, Art:** Searched for corresponding photos of famous people and even copies of real ads, paintings and movie posters

- **Typing and Computer Skills:** Typed all text

- **Spelling and Grammar:** Edited and proofread text

- **Graphic Design:** Experimented with fonts

- **Newspaper Writing:** Wrote headlines and captions

- **Newspaper Page Design:** Paginated text into newspaper columns and re-sized photos to fit

All of the students—even the kindergartener—participated in this project. Because they each made their own newspaper, I gave them freedom to not only choose the topics but to choose how they would express the information on the page.

Each student designed their newspaper to fit their skill level and talents. For example, one student loves to draw, so he included original artwork; the oldest was ready for a good writing challenge, so he had the most articles; and the five-year-old just wanted to make art about flappers, fashion and jazz, so hers was more of a poster board than a newspaper.

Newspaper content was developed as we studied the different subtopics of the 1920s. It took us several weeks to gather the content—reading lots of books, writing essays and collecting photos and art along the way. Then we took several days for newspaper assembly. It was such a great way for the kids to link subject knowledge and skills, and for them to create a tangible expression of all they'd learned!

Action Plan:

1. Have you seen evidence that your perfectly planned homeschool schedule has caused angst between you and your kids? Is the joy of homeschooling gone (for you and/or your kids) because learning has become forced? If so, re-read the chapter. Examine the areas that cause the most tension, and pray for God to show you why the tension exists. Consider implementing other "back door" teaching methods like games until such time that the love of learning is re-established.

2. Have you witnessed moments of exploratory learning when you let go of the schedule and just let students explore a topic? If not, give it a try one day.

3. Choose a student activity or project that allows students to learn about several subjects at once. See what kind of learning enfolds as you experiment with blurring the lines between subjects, and thus, between scheduled subject times.

CHAPTER 10:

When Life Interrupts Your "Perfect" Schedule

You've had this moment too. In fact, you probably have it one magical day a year. You open your eyes to the morning light. As your brain wakes up and begins thinking through the day, you suddenly remember: *today's my birthday!*

That was the pleasant scene I woke up to on a Tuesday in late winter 2008.

I was still laying on my back, adrift in the pleasure of the moment (*It's my birthday! My BIRTHDAY!*) when I heard a little voice from the side of the bed.

"Momma, I itchy," it said simply.

I sat up and found my three-and-a half-year-old covered in angry, bright-red blotches and puffed up like a marshmallow.

I nudged my still-sleeping husband (well, he probably woke up when he heard me gasp and shout "Oh my gosh!" at the sight of our son). Nevertheless, he instantly rolled over and took in the scene.

Incredulous, we both stood there with our mouths open. *What in the world?!* As we examined him more closely, fully awake now, we began going through the scenarios: No one we knew had chicken pox. It had been cold lately, so the kids had barely been outside, let alone played near bushes that might have caused a rash.

And then we noticed he wasn't breathing well either. Gasping and wheezing was more like it. Not quite call-911-status, but definitely not normal.

We immediately called the doctor. We were told to bring him in right away.

That was the day we discovered he was allergic to penicillin. An emergency visit to the doctor, a child covered in a strange, scary rash, and then a lesson in how to apply an oxygen mask to a three-and-a-half year-old. Yeah, **not exactly how I'd dreamt of spending my birthday**.

Or the next seven days. We spent almost every day that week at the doctor's office as the allergic reaction—and the subsequent hives, swelling and wheezing—raged through his poor little body. He'd been on penicillin for eight days before showing signs, so it took a very long time for the symptoms to pass. There were several times in that week when we almost admitted him to the hospital. When we weren't at the doctor or at home pumping him full of Benadryl, we kept him in a cool bath—basically the only thing that kept the itching moderately at bay.

My sweet, mellow boy was exhausted mentally and physically and just wanted it to be over. After five days of this craziness, one afternoon he just began crying uncontrollably. I held him close, tears streaming down my cheeks too. He was a wreck, and so was I.

I think it goes without saying that we did very little homeschool that week. In fact, I think the only "school" I did was reading a few stories aloud while sitting at the doctor's office.

This situation wasn't planned and it wasn't ideal. But, unfortunately, it was our reality that week.

Now That's One Upset Apple Cart

We do our best to prepare for life's interruptions (which is why we included "free time" in our schedule). But darn it, life doesn't just interrupt from 1:00-3:00 pm on a Thursday afternoon like we may have scheduled.

These disruptions can be sudden, jarring and life-altering.

Sometimes they last for a day or for a week. Sometimes they last the entire school year (or longer).

Here are a few examples of those "big" interruptions that can rock your world (and your schedule):

- Your husband just lost his job and you need to get a part-time job ASAP (while still homeschooling your children).

- Your teenage nephew just committed suicide and your sister is beside herself with grief.

- A tornado ripped through your town yesterday afternoon, severely damaging your home.

111

- Your mother-in-law is moving in due to a recent stroke.

- You just learned that your neighbor has Stage 3 Breast Cancer and you offered to help watch her kids three days a week.

How are we expected to maintain any semblance of a schedule during these challenging times?

Ever heard the phrase, "The baby *is* the lesson"? It means that the real lesson to be learned in a given situation is found in the very thing that is causing the disruption.

I'm grateful that my family has not endured enormously difficult situations like the ones stated above. However, we have gone through many small speed bumps where I have seen this "the baby is the lesson" principle repeatedly ring true. These difficulties may only last for a day at a time, but they repeat themselves over and over, making me ask myself, "Am I stuck in *Groundhog Day* (remember that old Bill Murray movie)? Geez, can I just learn the lesson already?!"

As teachers, we tend to forget that *we* are students too! God wants to teach us and sometimes he has to **shake us from our boxed-in routines so that he can provide a time of growth and change**.

Instead of being angry and frustrated about our upset little apple cart, what if we stepped back from the situation and asked ourselves, "What can I (and my kids) learn in this situation? What unique life lessons is God trying to teach us?"

It's kind of like when I hear my kids pray for character traits like "obedience" or "perseverance." I smile inside, knowing how our wonderful Father-Creator-Teacher likes to gift those qualities to us: through challenging circumstances.

So if I hear them praying for specific character traits, I tell them to **watch out for "God-sightings."**

"Our God is a gentleman," I say. "He won't make us act a certain way in a situation. But, he will give you lots of opportunities to practice the right behavior."

I remind them of this when I hear them praying for the trait, and again when the God-sighting appears: "Do you remember what you were praying for this morning? This is God's attempt to let you practice that new behavior. **Are you going to make the choice to practice the correct behavior and learn the lesson quickly, or will God have to keep presenting these situations to you?"**

And of course, there are situations where God wants to perfect our character—even if we didn't specifically ask for the "perfecting."

All of this is to say that "interruptions" to the schedule—planned or unplanned—have a purpose, and that growing time for us is often a growing time for our kids as well.

While this growing time may not be traditional textbook learning, these experiences are invaluable and just as educational! Remember— they help accomplish those big-picture goals that you just can't find a textbook for: stuff like developing family connections, building

Christ-like character and cultivating necessary life skills. Roll with the punches and look for the lesson.

When God Gives You A New Lesson Plan

In spring of 2012, my mom needed to have an unexpected surgery. My dad wasn't able to take any time off work. My sister, my only sibling, lives five minutes from my mom, but she also works full-time. It was smack dab in the middle of our school year, my parents live more than two hours away and, quite frankly, our schedule was fairly full. But I knew my mom would need help, and I saw a **unique opportunity to teach my kids about the importance of service.**

So we ditched our homeschool schedule and all our plans. My four-year-old daughter, my still-nursing infant son and I traveled to my mom's house and set up camp for the week. The older boys stayed behind with my husband who worked from home (I didn't want to overwhelm my recovering mom with four kids!).

While we were gone, the boys still maintained a very loose homeschool framework—Bible in the morning, Math, and lots of independent reading. I also asked them to please spend time each day praying for their nana's speedy recovery and that my daughter and I would be able to humbly display God's love for her while we were there.

True, my daughter was only four at the time, but she possesses a beautiful, compassionate spirit that longs to serve and to take care of others. This future nurse is always the first on the scene to comfort those who are hurt and to offer a big hug and a Band-Aid. What an excellent opportunity for her to share and grow her unique God-given talents! **This was real-world, applied learning—for a preschooler!**

These unscheduled opportunities are some of the greatest beauties in homeschooling. Look for them! They remind me of the story of the Good Samaritan in Luke 10:30-37. We've got to be open to dropping our preconceived schedules so that we can enjoy the spontaneous learning that God has planned!

Character Development Doesn't Keep A Schedule

Recently the kids and I were getting ready for an all-day field trip. My older sons were finishing up some math before we left, and my daughter and I were in the kitchen. I was gathering up sunscreen and other last-minute items. Lunches still needed to be made, and we were running behind schedule.

It was also my daughter's scheduled math time, but I decided it would really help us if she could quickly put together the lunches for everyone. She had very little math to do that day, honestly, and I figured she could accomplish both tasks before we go. Plus, the kids and I had been talking lately about looking for opportunities to serve one another. So I saw burrito making as a spontaneous lesson in character building (math could be done at any time).

My usually helpful daughter gave me a look. One of *those* looks. "Do I have to make ones for the boys too?"

"Yes, please," I said. "It would really help us get out the door faster."

She still was not convinced. **"What am I, their servant?"** she said, in an irritated, arrogant tone.

Her response shocked me out of my bustling around. *Oh, yes. God was definitely presenting me with one of those time-sensitive teaching moments.* Summoning up my patience (and doing my best to respond gently with a controlled tongue), I crouched down so that we were at eye level. **"Yes, exactly. You are their servant."**

I paused. I could tell by her eyes that she was surprised at my response.

I continued. "I am your servant, and you are my servant too. God calls us to love and to serve each other. He says that a person that lays down his life for someone else shows the greatest love to that person." I then shared how Jesus was the greatest example of this in how he gave up his entire life to love and to serve others.

We continued the discussion while she worked. We talked about the joys that come when we serve, especially when that service is unsolicited or done quietly without asking for acknowledgment. We talked about how God says that everything that we do should be done as if we were working for God himself, no matter how mundane or meaningless it seemed.

Did she miss math that day? Yep. The food preparation took longer than anticipated because I also asked her to gather up the drinks and the snacks. But, as she was working, **we enjoyed a priceless teaching moment that was infinitely more valuable.**

Moms, we must not be so locked in our schedules that we cannot be available to connect with our kids about the deeper, more important topics of life. These times to speak into our child's heart can't be scheduled or planned for.

Running A Household Doesn't Have To Be An Interruption

The longer I homeschool (and the more kids I have) the more I'm reminded of the importance of being organized. Well, more than just organized: **orderly and methodical in my household maintenance.**

Want to know a huge secret about homeschooling that no one tells you? When you get on top of the rest of your household duties— creating a scheduled time and method for accomplishing each— your homeschool days will be infinitely smoother. When you know that the laundry, grocery shopping, housecleaning and dishes will be accomplished at certain times in your day or week, you can peacefully homeschool without worrying if those necessary evils will get done. **They will get done, because you've created systems to manage these tasks,** and these systems have been added as "anchors" to your schedule.

These tasks are simply enfolded into our homeschool day. For example, washing and folding laundry is as much a part of our Monday routine, in the same way Bible is at 8:00 a.m. and Math is at 9:00 a.m.

If you find that **homemaking tasks are stealing your planned school time, go back to your schedule and see how you have (or have not)**

planned for laundry, chores and the like. Chapters 7 and 8 talk about this in more detail. Also, check out "Additional Helpful Resources" in the Appendix for books that can help you create these systems for household maintenance.

"Schoolwork" Still Needs To Get Done!

True, a flexible schedule is great because life's interruptions are inevitable (and these challenges can be incredible learning experiences in themselves).

But thankfully a majority of our unplanned schedule interruptions won't be huge life-altering events. They will be simple things like nursing a sick child, appointments that need to be scheduled during school hours, or quickly cleaning up the house before a last-minute play date.

However, these **little interruptions can add up—even de-railing our progress** through a subject. That's a big problem because we've made a commitment to the state that we will teach our kids the mandated school subjects. We must be faithful to this promise and stay on track to meet those state-mandated goals.

Bottom line: How can we still get our traditional schoolwork done within the realities of everyday life?

One-time occurrence or bigger issue? This is the first question I ask. If you notice that school always gets disrupted around 10:00 a.m., for example, ask yourself why. **Is something happening within the**

family dynamics to produce this disruption? If a child becomes super squirmy at a specific time of the day (or during a specific subject), that's your clue to either give him a break or to give him more kinesthetic activities at that time.

Or here's another example. You find that your normally content four-year-old becomes very irritated after lunch on Thursday afternoons, especially during the times when you're trying to help the older kids through their weekly Science experiments. Each week, she clings to you and disrupts the teaching time with her attention-grabbing behavior. You examine the schedule and realize that she is often left to play alone on Thursday mornings because those are the times when you teach the older girls key writing concepts. How can you re-arrange the schedule to give your younger daughter some one-on-one time on Thursdays (thereby reducing the behavior issues and allowing the schoolwork to continue)?

Shorten or modify the lesson. If you notice a pattern of bad behavior, complaining and grouchiness around a particular subject, it's time to take a closer look at what's happening. **Is the learning approach** (or the way the kids respond to the information, such as essay writing or oral narration) **working**? Maybe you're just trying to cover too much. Consider consolidating subjects or topics. Take inventory of the situation and determine if the lesson needs to be condensed or modified for the sake of the learning environment.

More than anything, trust the homeschooling process. This is *not* traditional schooling with its 8:00 a.m. to 2:30 p.m. time constraints! It is a blessing that we aren't required to define school as learning that occurs *only* within these hours! We're developing life-long learners.

119

Our goal is to give them a love of learning and to let them run with it—in whatever ways available on a given day.

Thankfully, we are given the freedom to let learning follow in a more realistic pattern and to insert creative solutions to our day (if need be) to get that learning in. Here are a few strategies to tackle those infrequent interruptions.

Go mobile and get the work done on the road. This is where workbooks really shine. I personally don't like to over-use a workbook, but if we need to be out and about, it's a no-fuss easy way to get the work done.

If kids are older, **they can do almost anything (short of a hands-on experiment or a messy art project) on the road**. Thanks to internet-filtered laptops, phones and tablets, they can research projects, write essays—you name it.

Tablets and phones are also great for teaching younger kids on-the-go. My iPad is filled with tons of interactive readers and games for phonics, writing, geography, math—**activities to match nearly every subject we study**. It's a fun treat for the kids, and also a great way to review concepts.

I encourage you to **stay on top of the latest educational games and apps** by subscribing to homeschooling blogs like "Apps for Homeschooling" or even following my Pinterest "iPad Apps for Learning" Board. Many of these apps are free or only a few dollars. We'll talk more about using these alternative teaching resources in Chapter 11.

Skip the lesson or subject for the day. Accept the fact that you may have a light homeschool day or week. We can't do this every week of course, but sometimes you just can't fit it all in, and that's alright. There's a natural ebb-and-flow to homeschooling: some weeks are heavy on the learning, and other weeks are light. On these days, we have to trust the process that overall we're making strides toward our learning goals.

Say no to something else in order to get it done. If it's imperative that something's completed today or this week, consider saying no to another subject or commitment. The fact is that there's only so much time in a day, and if we say yes to one thing, sometimes we have to say no to something else. That's just reality.

If nothing else, read aloud to your kids. I can't tell you how many times we've sat in a doctor's examining room and read history or science books (either as read alouds or independent readers). Kids can learn so much when they simply read (or are read to)! In fact, there are entire curriculums like *Five In A Row* based around this concept.

If we've had a tough day and not much "school" has gotten done, the kids and I snuggle around a good book. It centers us as a family, grounds us back to our homeschool commitments, and (a nice benefit) it imparts an incredible amount of information. I find that reading aloud is like a soothing balm on those rough days.

Reading aloud can also be **an effective strategy for those longer seasons when the schedule is disrupted.** My friend Katelin shares about a unique season in her homeschooling. When she was on bed rest while pregnant with her fourth child, she read extensively to her second grader, kindergartener and three year old. Because she spent her days in bed or on the couch, she termed it "couchschooling":

> Whatever I could do from the couch, we did. Along with lots of children's literature, I read them The Burgess Animal Book and Christian Liberty Presses' history readers. My second grader read aloud to me and to the other children. They learned a lot that year, especially in science, because I took the time to field their questions and to have discussions. We would also play games like "find me something that starts with the letter G" or for my three-year-old I'd say "go find me three yellow things." What else was I going to do? I was stuck on the couch or in bed!

I love this story because it reminds me that if life throws my schedule a major curveball, learning can still be accomplished by simply reading to my kids.

Action Plan:

1. How do you react to the expected and unexpected interruptions to your schedule?

2. Do you see a pattern in schedule interruptions? If so, ask God to show you what he might be trying to teach you (or your child).

3. Are your household responsibilities disrupting your homeschool schedule? If so, take a second look at the systems you may (or may not) have in place to handle these everyday tasks. What needs to be changed? Do you need to allocate more time to the schedule for these tasks? Are there tasks that the children can be regularly responsible for?

CHAPTER 11:

A Living Curriculum For Real, Live Kids

"Oh my goodness," I cooed, in my best southern belle voice. "Do tell us about the horrific fighting you've endured!" I fanned myself with my daughter's homemade fan for added effect.

My third-grade son, clothed in his "finest" Civil War military gear, adjusted his military-issued rifle (AKA his BB gun).

"Well, ma'am," he began, his eyes downcast and his countenance serious. "Some of the battles have been incredibly rough. That one at Gettysburg was really terrible and we lost a lot of men."

"Frankly, it was..." he began in earnest, and then stopped himself. He leaned in close and stated soberly, "Well, you ladies don't need to know the details of the horrors of war."

I laughed out loud, almost choking on my sip of strawberry lemonade.

"Mom!" he said, suddenly becoming my nine-year-old son again. "You can't laugh! We have to stay in character here!"

Oh my word, I thought. *How am I supposed to be Mary Lincoln when you're cracking me up with these comments?!*

We were seated in our backyard on an old picnic blanket. **My older boys were dressed as Union generals; my daughter was pretending** to be a woman of high society, and, yes, I was the First Lady (and host of our "strawberry soiree"), Mrs. Mary Lincoln.

We'd made as many "strawberry things" as we could think of (strawberry salad, strawberry lemonade, strawberry shortcake, chocolate-covered strawberries), dressed in our makeshift period costumes (my three-year-old daughter's outfit had a striking resemblance to a certain Disney Princess), and had a great time pretending to live in Civil War America.

This incredibly fun afternoon—easily one of the highlights of that school year—hadn't been planned back in September when we'd begun the school year. In fact, **I'd come up with the concept only a week earlier when we had learned a random fact about Abraham and Mary Lincoln: they loved to throw a good party, especially a "strawberry soiree."** In fact, the Lincolns were famous for these parties where practically every dish contained strawberries.

I had wanted to find a **fun, low-stress way to review our five-week unit on the Civil War**, and hosting our own "strawberry soiree" seemed like just the ticket. It had just been a bonus that strawberries were on sale that week.

I share this story because it exemplifies how sometimes our best learning activities aren't planned months in advance. **Sometimes they just come together while the learning process is in motion.**

The One-Size-Fits-None Curriculum Plan

My first foray into the homeschooling life involved a certain curriculum that gave a highly detailed list of daily activities (down to the exact pages to read each day). **I was told that this was supposed to "free" me, because now I didn't need to create my own school schedule.** "Think of all the extra time you'll have because you won't be planning daily lessons!" the curriculum brochure promised.

It all sounded good until I actually started going through the curriculum and realized that my family—or anyone's family, for that matter—could not perfectly accomplish the schedule the curriculum had laid out! Although the curriculum itself was challenging and filled with quality material, **I found it extremely difficult to discern daily assignments because our days *never perfectly matched up* with what the curriculum had scheduled for us.**

I'd see that there was a great assignment on Thursday for Science, but then realize (based on the flow of today's class conversation) how much better it would be to do it today. But the problem was that today was Tuesday and I was supposed to be doing something else today for Science. *No problem,* I'd say, *I'll just switch the days and do today's assignment on Thursday. It's no big deal to switch things up now and then.*

But I quickly saw that this switching wasn't happening "now and then." **Instead, I was switching assignments around on a daily basis.** Sometimes I'd find a great idea outside the curriculum that I wanted to include too. I'd need to find a home for it in the schedule, which meant more switching and some eliminating. Then, as luck would have it, a cold or the flu would sweep through our family and we'd need to spend a few days *off* our schedule resting and recuperating. What happened to the assignments on those days?

Suddenly, I was asking myself, *What happened to my "pre-planned" schedule? **How is this giving me extra time?***

Was this the curriculum's fault per se? Not really. While the curriculum wasn't my favorite, it had decent content.

The problem was that the curriculum's rigid schedule pigeonholed my week into an awkwardly-sized, unworkable shape. **Like an oddly-sized garment that was loose in some areas and tight in others, this one-sized-all, pre-fixed schedule was clearly one-size-fits-none.** I was tired of the extra time I spent tailoring this supposedly "time-saving schedule" to fit my family's natural learning flow.

What I really needed was a **detailed subject plan that was organized and purposeful, yet flexible enough to allow for exploratory learning, last-minute project ideas and the occasional hiccup in our week.**

Build An Organized Yet Flexible Subject Plan

It took me several years, but eventually I transitioned into a new way of organizing my curriculum plans. It has revolutionized our class time and brought so much freedom.

Instead of a moment-by-moment daily schedule of pre-determined curriculum content, I create a **"Subject Plan": a document that outlines the general topics for each subject, and lists a range of potential activities for those topics.** I let our days naturally determine the actual assignments.

Let's take Science as an example. Let's say I'm going to cover Anatomy this year.

First, I come up with **a rough list of the content to cover** such as "the Brain and Nervous System," "the Heart and Circulatory System," "the Lungs and Respiratory System" and so on. Preferably, this topical list would at least partially come from a main science textbook on Anatomy. I consider this main textbook my "spine" or "core curriculum" for the subject.

Then, using the dates from my Master School Calendar, **I create an Excel document**—which I title "(Subject Name) Subject Plan"—that **lists these topics by our planned school weeks. Each topic and corresponding school week would get a row in the document.** "The Brain and Nervous System" might become September 1-12 (week one and two of our school year), while "the Heart and Circulatory System" is assigned to September 15-26 (weeks three and four).

Next, I create **a list of the types of activities and resources that could teach these topics.** Of course this includes my "spine," but it also contains additional supplemental resources. **I create columns within the document to house each of these different learning avenues:** "Supplemental Books," "Websites," "Online games/iPad Apps," "Online Videos/Movies," "Field Trips," etc.

Then, I begin plugging ideas into the schedule. This is where the treasure hunt begins! While a strong curriculum core provides much of the content ideas, I enjoy digging around to find other unique ways to learn a topic. So, for example, if I find a great online video of how the heart beats, I would paste the link in the column "Online Videos/Movies" in the row that contains the topic "The Heart and Circulatory System." The name of a pop-up book about the division of the brain would be filed under the column "Supplemental Books," in the row "The Brain and Nervous System," and so on. You could include as many additional details here as you like, for example: "pages 14-18," "library book to borrow," "Netflix movie," or "buy this book on Amazon."

A Growing And Changing Subject Plan

The key here is not to reach a point where you state, "I have gathered absolutely every resource and curriculum idea for this subject." **Instead, have specific "gathering" periods throughout the year, storing and gathering ideas in the Subject Plan document as you go.** Here's how I do it.

In the summer, as part of my annual school planning, I gather the core school books and determine the main topics we want to cover. If there's a supplemental resource that I know we will use for multiple weeks, I consider purchasing it as well. At this time, I also try to plug in as many ideas as possible into the subject plan, especially for the topics covered in the first month or two of school.

Like a parent pushing a child on his first two-wheeled bike ride, these activities give me a good push toward what will happen this year.

A few weeks before we start a new topic, I intensify my "activity gathering" process again. This is when I look online again for resources, review the specific books available at my library and gather ideas.

Right before the week begins, I review what topic we'd planned to cover and the ideas I've gathered. I make an extremely loose structure of how the activities might work out that week: "On Monday, let's read from our core book about Western Expansionism in the 1850s and talk about questions on page 118; on Wednesday let's make a map that details the Oregon Trail and play an online game; on Thursday, let's build a covered wagon from an idea I've got on my 'Homeschooling: History' Pinterest Board."

The week may work out exactly like this...or it may not! This is a general outline and if something isn't working, you can always switch in another activity from your Subject Plan that might work better.

Your Ideas Are A Like A Buffet. Don't Overeat!

You don't have to do everything on your list. **Like the items at an "all-you-can-eat" buffet, you don't need to fill your days with absolutely every item from your Subject Plan.** Really.

When my family visits a certain soup-and-salad buffet restaurant nearby, we're never quite sure what we'll eat. We do know we'll build our own salads and have the restaurant's tasty focaccia bread (which my children refer to as "pizza"). But sometimes there's a great soup I want to try. Or on some occasions my husband opts for fresh fruit for dessert instead of his typical caramel sundae. It depends on our individual moods and in what options are available.

It's the same thing with your Subject Plan. Give yourself lots of choices for what may work. **Gather ideas throughout the year—the new ideas along with those tried and true learning methods—and pick activities as you go.** Options are a good thing!

Most importantly, **don't make it your goal to complete every project idea!** Just like cleaning out the buffet is not the goal when dining at an all-you-can-eat restaurant, **completing everything on your Subject Plan is not a true measure of successfully teaching a topic.** Instead, ask yourself, "Did the child connect with the material in a meaningful way? Did they gain knowledge and express it in ways that will help them retain that information?" *These* are the true marks of "successfully learning" a given topic. Chances are that you'll eventually cycle through this topic again in your homeschool, and when you do, you can try those ideas then.

Additional Tips for Tailoring a Subject Plan to Fit

You can create these types of Excel Spreadsheets for each subject you cover. Or...not. **Some subjects are super easy to plan and may just consist of working through a single book or curriculum without any additional outside resources.**

Pick and choose the subjects where you really want to have multiple learning options. **Don't make yourself crazy and do this for every single subject, especially with multiple kids!**

By the way, **if you are teaching the same topics to several children at the same time (but the children are in very different levels of their schooling), consider creating a unique subject spreadsheet for each learning level.** This isn't really necessary for kids that are close in grade level. **I'm talking to the moms with, say, a second grader and a high schooler.** True, it adds additional complexity and work to make unique subject spreadsheets for each child, but it also gives specific options for all the learning levels present in your classroom which gives you freedom and choices for when it's time to teach.

Why A Living, Growing Subject Plan?

It leaves room for your kids' growth and new interests. Last spring, my son enjoyed a short foray into watercolors. He attended an art camp in late March where he spent several days playing around in this beautiful art medium. So when we studied the Wild West not long after, he begged me to allow him to paint a western mountain scene as his main project for the history unit.

It gives kids options. Your kids may not want to create a clay sculpture of the Titanic (even though they loved creating ones for the *Niña, Pinta* and the *Santa Maria* when you talked about "New World Explorers" six months ago). Kids can be weird and unpredictable in what they will like (but aren't we like that too as adults from time to time?). Having a plethora of options available to cover a topic gives

133

freedom for those days when a child is particular about what he does and does not want to do.

It allows for last-minute ideas and plans to be easily added. I find many of those spur-of-the-moment ideas online and Pinterest is an incredible place to gather and store them! You can keep separate boards for each subject, or even for topics within a subject. As you see great ideas online (either in the Pinterest feed or anywhere else), use the "Pin It" icon to add the link to your virtual Pinterest board. Then, anytime you need new ideas, simply open your board! If you need inspiration, you are welcome to follow my Pinterest Boards.

It allows for exploratory learning. Kids come up with great questions and that can lead to awesome spontaneous learning ideas.

When we recently learned about the circulatory system, I'd planned to only briefly mention how everyone's blood is a different type. However, the kids were fascinated by the fact that we each have different *kinds* of blood, so we spent a lot of time on it that day. "What type of blood do I have?" they asked. "What about Nana and Papa? Do we know anyone that has Type AB-negative blood (the rarest type)?" We made a chart of our family and had a lengthy discussion about who could give blood to whom. The kids wanted to know, "How the blood got inside someone else," and if it hurt to give blood away. While I explained the procedure as much as possible, I made a mental note to take them with me the next time I gave blood (for a real learning adventure)!

It allows flexibility for planned resources that may not be available. There have been many times that a curriculum recommended a particular read aloud or project book, but that resource wasn't available. This is especially true when trying to locate books through the library system. Sometimes there's a high demand for a book and it won't become available until after you're done covering the topic! **That's when I look for similar resources or search my Subject Plan for other ways to learn the information.** It's wonderful to not be locked into a particular supplemental book if it is not available.

Overall, having a Subject Plan provides structured and purposeful learning (important in helping us reach those annual or big-picture goals we've outlined) without the constraints of a predetermined, moment-by-moment plan. **It is a living, flexible way to effectively organize and plan curriculum.**

Action Plan:

1. Consider how you currently organize your daily curriculum assignments. Does your curriculum come with a pre-planned schedule, and if so, has that been a help or a hindrance?

2. Determine the subjects that will require the use of a Subject Plan. Begin listing out weekly topics and dates, along with the activities or resources to teach those topics.

3. How do you gather and organize homeschool ideas? Consider using Pinterest as a way to categorize and sort projects, online games, and online videos.

(Note: Check out the "Resources for Supplemental Curriculum" list in the Appendix for curriculum helps and learning resources that have helped our family).

Chapter 12:

Homeschooling With Joy And Freedom

Homeschooling has taught me to love disorder.

To love a messy stained countertop scattered with acrylic paint bottles, broken pieces of artist pastels, half-used watercolor pencils and partially completed canvases because that means that **a child experimented with several different art mediums to express himself.**

To see a desk crowded with stacks of paper, each filled with pictures, typed words and handwritten text: documented **proof of a young mind that's gathering and sorting through knowledge.**

To see eraser marks on paper because that means **a new piece of information was learned** and inserted to replace the previous information.

To see abandoned, half-created projects on my son's dresser because that means **he created something, learned from it and knew when it was time to move on** and try something else.

To hear my ten-year-old say, "Today I want to build a World War I bunker in the garage because I want to learn what it was like inside one," because that means **he hasn't given up on learning** and **he wants to express his knowledge outside of "school hours."**

It's taken me a long time to view these situations as **evidence of real learning (and not plain messiness in my home or mistakes in my scheduling).**

Real Learning Or Fact Recitation?

While, on the whole, learning can be organized and planned, real learning can also be impromptu and not follow an anticipated pattern.

It doesn't mean that real learning always finds a path away from the anticipated scheduled times. **Nor does it mean that we should abandon our schedules completely** because real learning can't happen within a purposefully-planned week.

Instead, it comes down to our view of what constitutes "real learning" and, subsequently, what parts of school we term as "successful" and "not successful." **Do we look at half-created projects and consider the assignment a failure? Do we view requests for different ways to express knowledge as annoyances** because they may require us to readjust the schedule for the week?

Real learning is radically different from fact recitation. Real learning means that **a person has fallen in love with knowledge, and has given themselves to a life of exploration and discovery.** Fact recitation is the opposite: a lifeless, temporary gathering of meaningless information.

138

Of course we want our kids to have real learning over fact recitation! But, some days, a scheduled learning time can become a hindrance to real learning.

What? Did she just say that scheduled learning times can hinder real learning… in a book about homeschool scheduling?

Well, yes… sort of. For more explanation, let's re-examine the "disorder" scenes I presented in the beginning of the chapter.

Real Learning Muddled In The Chaos

First, let's examine the scene of the various art paints, pastels and pencils in disarray. Maybe a student started with one art medium, saw they didn't like it, and started over with a new canvas and a new medium (thus the partially completed canvas). Or maybe a young artist decided to use a combination of several mediums on one canvas. It could have been that there were several students here, each starting with a different art medium, but as the class time progressed, they inspired each other to try a combination of all three mediums. **What was learned? Exploration, discovery and play through artistic expression.** But did all of that experimentation fit in the time scheduled for art? Maybe, maybe not.

Next, we see a desk crowded with stacks of paper, each filled with pictures, typed words and handwritten text. Information is being gathered and processed here. Sure, there's obviously been dedicated, scheduled time to gather the information. But what if some of the gathering happened outside the confines of class time? Maybe the child read additional books on the topic in their free time, or that the solution to a difficult equation *finally* came to them at 2 a.m. This tells us that **while pre-determined learning times are essential, the "aha" moments may come outside our regular schedule.**

What about the pencil eraser marks? This means a child may not have understood the information within the time allowed. The eraser marks and crossed out words on a page reveal how complex and individual the learning process can be. You planned to spend tomorrow's class time delving into the next topic, but **real learning may require that you plan a review time instead.**

Or there may be times when a child abandons a project. Do we push them to complete it? Or do we allow them to try a different method for knowledge expression, even if pursuing a different avenue for expression will result in a change in schedule and curriculum planning? Maybe they simply got bored or distracted and they need to be encouraged to finish. Or maybe the project is too hard, too complicated or not the right fit for their learning style and they need to try something else. There is no right answer here, but **real learning requires that you take the time to consider the correct solution.**

Lastly, there are those wonderful moments when a child embraces what he's been learning and wants to do additional study. When my ten-year-old talks about creating a life-size setup of something that we've been studying (such as the World War I bunker), I have two choices: to be annoyed by the potentially huge mess he may make; or to be excited for him because he's catching the vision for real learning. Either way, **this additional study will probably be outside the prescribed class times.**

In these moments, **we have to make the call** as to where adherence to a schedule is important; or whether we take a deep breath and allow this type of real learning to slightly alter the schedule's direction.

We have to be wise enough to see these opportunities, and, brave enough to adjust our schedule, if necessary, to let real learning happen.

The Curse Of The "Shoulds," "Musts" And "Have Tos"

Remember that I told you I did a lot of forced learning when I began my homeschooling journey? I had sacrificed my sons' love of learning for the sake of my need to stay "on schedule." **I used a lot of "shoulds," "musts" and "have tos" back in those days.** It wasn't pretty and it definitely wasn't real learning. Eventually they rebelled against school and wanted nothing to do with "school" learning. I had to back way off and start over.

Homeschooling joy and freedom came for me when I found **the happy balance of scheduled and unscheduled learning**. It came when I determined that I wanted real learning (not fact recitation) for my kids, and that I was willing to adjust and even sacrifice my schedule some days to achieve it.

Today it's true that most of what would be termed "school time" for our family is fairly predictable and on a daily schedule. **But now I am willing to sometimes let those days get a little messy.**

I am willing to let things—even my schedule—get disorderly from time to time if it means we're generally following the learning course.

I am willing to try new things—and to let my kids experiment—even if it results in a mistake.

I am willing to put my relationship with my kids before my desire that they absorb every fact I present.

I have decided to get off the safe, always-scheduled learning path and to ride the exhilarating roller coaster of real, unabashed discovery (which exists both inside and outside the schedule).

I haven't thrown out the schedule, not by any means (which is why several chapters of this book are dedicated to formulating schedules). **I just use it more wisely now—as a guide, not a prison.**

The Fallacy Of A "Complete" School Year

In late spring and early summer, a strange phenomenon happens for us homeschoolers. Others—especially those outside of the homeschooling community—begin asking us, **"Are you done with school yet?"** We get the opposite question in the fall: **"When are you going back to school?"**

It seems a strange concept to delineate "school" (especially something as natural as homeschooling) as having a start or stop date. Yet every year, in the late spring and early fall, we must field these questions.

Does anyone else see this definition of "today is a school day and tomorrow is not" as somewhat ridiculous?

Of course I understand the purpose behind the questions. Our society has been conditioned to the concept of a September to June school year, with a specific "break" from school in the summer months. The state must have some way of ensuring that kids are spending a certain percentage of their days in a year "doing school," and these days must be quantifiable on a calendar. **This results in a nice, orderly system for determining when school is "in," and when school is "out."**

Unfortunately, it can be ridiculous (and downright inaccurate) to label learning as happening only within these quandrants. **This is especially true if you're trying to gift kids with the joy of lifelong learning** because, by its very definition, learning doesn't have a "starting" and "stopping" point.

As we finish a school year, **don't we all undergo a petering "in" and "out" of what would be called "traditional" study times?**

During those last few weeks of May and in early June, I make goals and plans (and still generally live by the schedule) but I also begin a gradual transition of letting them all go.

We still complete our 175 required school days (*I promise, State Board of Education!*), but during this season those days are more relaxed. They are an unpredictable blend of, one day, lots of traditional "classroom" learning (as we finish up our projects and goals for the year) and, the next day, time with friends exploring outside (which I believe is just a different form of learning). **Eventually this pattern becomes more play time and less traditional learning time.** And then one day the kids say, "Mom, are we out of school yet?" and I say something like, "once we've finished this last part of our project, yes, we are done."

Does this mean that learning ends when our last day of school comes? Hardly! Truth be told, all homeschoolers probably do much, much more learning than our "required" school days. Think of all that summer holds: camping, trips to the beach or the lake, playing outside, hiking… the 19th century educator Charlotte Mason would call this "Nature Study" at its finest! And of course there's the summer reading programs and themed camps (such as Vacation Bible School, Sports Camps, Art Camps, etc) that many of our kids participate in.

The world outside our four walls is just *begging us* for discovery, especially this time of year. Like a woman with a beautiful new dress, the world in late spring and early summer is proudly on display and alive with color. The weather is warming, butterflies flutter through our backyards, flowers are in full bloom, lovely bird songs fill the air, and (thankfully) the days are longer to enjoy it all.

It's almost as if God himself is saying, "Come on out of your schoolbooks! Look at the magnificent, real beauty that I've created for this moment! Explore, learn and enjoy it all with me." **Of course, being outside and enjoying creation is magnificent any time of year, but it seems like nature calls us the most loudly during spring and summer.**

One of the homeschool bloggers I follow, Renee Tougas of Fun In My Backyard (fimby.tougas.net), lives in a rural part of Canada right next to the woods. In a post titled "Dropping It All," she describes how especially difficult it is for her family to stay inside during late spring (the time of year that most of us are ending our school year) and do what would be considered "traditional" schooling. As the world outside is awakened from its post-winter slushy state to a scene bursting with life and color, she and her children especially long to drop the schoolbooks and to go outside and to discover and embrace the beauty.

> *As our elementary school term ends, very unceremoniously, with the arrival of spring, I like to remind myself that a commitment to lifelong learning frees us from the need to start and end at certain times.*

> *It also frees us up from the need to complete the workbook, complete the lessons, complete the term. Learning does not reach completion. Discreet projects and courses may be completed but the learning and application of math, writing, reading, history, etc... are not something you "finish".*

> *During a season of school lessons (roughly fall and winter) I like having a plan to follow. I also like having this plan as a fall-back for those relaxed spring and summer months, on days or weeks when more direction and structure are needed.*

> *I love making school plans but those are always subject to... pretty much everything else. Subject to birthday weeks, subject to spring, subject to my inspiration and motivation, subject to... real life.*

> *And what I've learned through the years is that this is ok. It doesn't mean I am raising lazy, sloth children who will never apply*

themselves. It means I'm raising lifelong learners who know that learning is not limited to school lessons and textbooks.

I really love how she describes this delicate, slow fade of the schedule into the relaxing (yet still learning-filled) days of summer. **It really is difficult to, as she describes it, "'wrap up' a homeschooling year nice and tidy, like a package with a bow."**

I would add that it's also difficult (and unnecessary) to "finish" a book or particular curriculum by the end of a school year. Again, we all feel the "push" to finish that workbook or finishing our outlined objectives for the year. But if we succumb to this temptation, forced learning is almost always the result.

We needn't beat ourselves up for not "finishing" all that we'd outlined for the year. It's ludicrous that we should expect ourselves to perfectly outline in September what we will finish by June! And it's even more ridiculous to expect a pre-planned curriculum to accurately determine if we've "finished" for the year or not.

Instead, let's commit to working heartily toward our learning goals throughout the year, and then allow ourselves the freedom to say "nope, that's enough for now" at the end. You may spend two years going through a set of topics that was "supposed" to only take one year; or you may only cover half of the topics in a given curriculum. That's fine! The real question shouldn't be "Did we finish the curriculum?" but "Did quality learning take place during the year? Have the children progressed in their knowledge and skills in this area?"

There's no need to unnecessarily rush the learning. Remember, the information will always be there next year!

A Gentle Return To Formal Instruction

In addition, I would argue that **our transition back *into* our school schedule be more than (using Renee's "unwrapping a package" analogy from above), a mad dash to rip open a beautifully wrapped gift.**

We just spent the majority of this book in preparation: reviewing what was working and not working; getting input from our kids on what they want to learn and how they want to learn it; investigating curriculum; calculating the arbitrary beginning and end of our school year; and formulating a weekly plan. What is the result of all this difficult work? The priceless, ornately wrapped gift of a potentially incredible homeschool year!

Why do we feel inclined to rush ourselves (and our children) into it? **Why do we want to hastily rip off the wrapping paper, hurriedly shove the gift into a child's hands and demand that they play with it?**

Perhaps we're excited to take these carefully chosen homeschool resources (the ones we've been poring over all summer!) finally out for a test drive on the open highway. Maybe we've greatly enjoyed our summer, but now we're longing for that comfort of a controlled schedule again, so we push, push, push our kids back into the routine. **Or perhaps we like having the documented evidence to show those**

well-intentioned homeschooling naysayers that *yes, the children are indeed receiving a fine education, thank you very much.*

Instead, what if we returned to our traditional school year schedule with as much flexibility as we let it go? Instead of pushing our kids off the diving board into the pool of learning (forcing them to quickly "sink or swim"), **what if we took the shallow-end-route into the pool and allowed them to gradually acclimate to the water?**

Remember that real learning is still happening (in various levels) when our kids are "off" school. When school begins again, we are simply changing the pace and returning to a more formal style of learning.

Going "back to school" doesn't have to be an abrupt, groan-inducing process, full of fights and tears. Think of it as a welcoming--**a gentle slow nudge that encourages more structured study, but still leaves room for the untraditional forms of learning they enjoyed over summer break.**

In the fall, as we begin the slow transition to a traditional school schedule, the world outside will reflect this pattern. Deciduous trees slowly begin the process of returning to winter hibernation, and the temperature outside begins to have a decided chill. There will be cooler days as autumn draws nigh, interspersed with the occasional warm spell. The shift from summer to winter is a slow and gradual one, reminding us that our return to scheduled learning can be slow and gradual too.

Most days we can explore the new curriculum and test out the waters of the schedule, but there are those days when we can still enjoy the informal learning style of summer. Eventually, the routine becomes more comfortable, it becomes easier to stay inside and we find ourselves back in that scheduled "school" routine—happily plugging away at our educational goals for the year.

Welcome To The Learning Life

Learning is a journey that begins the moment we take our first breath and ends the moment we take our last and pass into eternity. **Learning happens for a lifetime and it is a natural by-product of living.**

Thankfully, homeschooling allows us to set learning goals and to outline schedules for our children's first eighteen years of life. These are the years when our kids have the opportunity to fall in love with knowledge. During these years, our kids begin their exploration of the world around us—taking in all the past, present and future realities.

These are the years when we are called to help our children establish strong morals and a godly character foundation. Thankfully, homeschooling also gives room for character development we simultaneously schedule time for instructing our kids in righteousness and daily model godly character. Relationships and deep family bonds are developed during these times as well.

These high summits of homeschooling cannot be reached without long-term and yearly goal-setting, along with a commitment to purposeful living. This is life that, for the most part, is lived within the context of a schedule. **This planned life has a determined, persevering focus that make goals happen. It also has the wisdom to know when to drop those well-laid plans and to embrace the unexpected learning of the moment.**

It may not be a safe predictable life (and is often riddled with imperfection), but *it is the learning life*—**the passionately lived life of those who plan to be flexible.**

May you and your kids capture this beautiful vision for the learning life! It is my sincere prayer that the book's contents have encouraged you and that they have given you a plan and purpose for your homeschooling journey.

Action Plan:

1. How do you view "disorder" in your homeschool? Think through your everyday homeschool situations (like the ones detailed in the beginning of the chapter). Honestly assess how you view these situations. Do you see them as annoyances or disruptions to your "perfect" schedule? Instead, is it possible that real learning is happening here?

2. What does the transition "in" and "out" of a formal school schedule look like in your home? Consider how you and your children react to the change in school schedule. Is it a forced, immediate schedule implementation or a gradual fade in-and-out of the traditional school schedule?

Appendix

Assessment Questions:

What's Working... (And What's Not)?

About The Curricula/Learning Style:

1. Is real learning happening here? Do you see evidences of the child not only understanding the concepts but applying them in other school subjects and even in everyday conversation?

2. Does your child have an excitement to learn this subject? Does it come alive for them?

3. Do you battle with a child to complete a particular subject, and do you believe that the curricula may be partially to blame?

4. Do the curricula allow for the type of learning that you've chosen for your homeschool (for example, interest-led learning, literature-based learning, etc)?

5. Do the current curricula effectively teach the material for your students' grade level?

6. Are the curricula easy-to-follow and to understand (for both you and the student)?

7. Are accompanying resources easy to find?

8. Are you comfortable with the amount of preparation time required for the curriculum?

9. Are you content with the amount of hands-on teaching time required by the curriculum?

10. Does the student enjoy the curriculums? Do you see his love of learning broadening because of the curriculum?

About The Student(s):

1. What are his areas of weakness and areas of strength? What can you do to strengthen the weak areas?

2. Does he have a specific subject that he needs extra help in?

3. Are there core skills that you want him to learn by this time next year?

4. Does he need to review past-learned concepts?

5. Does he need assistance from outside sources (such as a tutor)?

6. Are there behavioral issues that need to be addressed?

7. What is the student's general attitude toward school?

8. Does he have adequate one-on-one teaching time with mom and independent learning time?

About The School Structure/Schedule:

1. Do the amount of school hours work for your students' needs and for the entire family schedule?

2. Will there be an expected life change next year (for example, a new baby, a planned move, a part-time job for mom) that will require a change in the annual homeschool schedule or in the daily hours of schooling?

3. Will a non-school aged child be changing to a new life stage that will require more attention (for example, a baby becoming a toddler)?

4. Should you consider adding additional out-of-the-home learning experiences, such as sports, clubs, or co-op teaching classes? Or do you participate in those experiences now and plan on eliminating them next year?

5. Are there non-traditional school subjects that you'd like to include? For example, this year would you like to teach your kids basic car maintenance or Plumbing 101? Are there new household skills such as folding laundry and cleaning windows that students need to learn? How do you plan to incorporate learning activities such as chores into the school day?

6. Does anything need to change in your classroom workspace (or other area where you do school) to facilitate learning?

7. Are there equipment, books, or software that need to be purchased to make learning easier?

8. Do you need to implement organizational tools or systems to streamline the school day?

9. What is the emotional tone of the classroom (Chaotic? Stressful? Creative? Frustrating? Relaxed?)? Is this in line with where you'd like it to be?

About The Teacher:

1. Are there things about your teaching style that you'd like to change?

2. Do you regularly exhibit the classroom behavior that you want your kids to have?

3. Would you choose you as your teacher?

4. If others also teach your child (such as in a co-op setting), are you content with their teaching style or do you need to look for new outside teaching resources?

Resources for Supplemental Curriculum

Here is a listing of some of our family's favorite supplemental learning resources. They can be additional learning resources to a main curriculum core, or they can be gathered together and made into a custom curriculum. Most are books and DVDs, but some are websites or blogs (all sites were working at time of publication). I found most of the books (and many DVDs) at my local library. Some of the video series or DVDs are available for free viewing if you subscribe to Netflix or can even be seen on YouTube.

I have also included some great resources for gathering ideas, including links to my Pinterest Boards.

Obviously this is not meant to be comprehensive list but a highlight of some supplemental resources that our family has enjoyed.

General (Multi-Disciplinary Resources):

Books:

- *Step Into Reading* books

- *DK Eyewitness* books

- Dover coloring books

- *Magic Tree House* book series and accompanying *Fact Tracker* books by Mary Pope Osborne

Websites/Blogs:

- Brain Pop (brainpop.com) (so many wonderful videos here for history, science, language, holidays—you name it. Each video topic has a quiz and supplemental activities. My kids love the videos on this site and we use it several times a week. It is a pay site, but some videos are free.)

- CurrClick.com (website that has lots of lapbooking and notebooking resources, many of them for instant download)

Math:

Books:

- *Math Wise! Over 100 Hands-On Activities that Promote Real Math Understanding, Grades K-8* by James L. Overholt and Laurie Kincheloe

- *Speed Math for Kids: The Fast, Fun Way to Do Math Calculations* by Bill Handley

- *Hands-On Math Projects With Real-Life Applications, Grades 6-12* by Judith A. and Gary Robert Muschla

- *The Greedy Triangle; Spaghetti and Meatballs for All!; The Book of Think: Or How to Solve A Problem Twice Your Size* and other math books by Marilyn Burns

- *Sir Cumference and the Viking's Map* and other Charlesbridge Math Adventures

- *Mummy Math: An Adventure in Geometry* and *Sir Cumference and the First Round Table* and other math books by Cindy Neushwander

- *Multiplying Menace: The Revenge of Rumpelstiltskin* and other math books by Pam Calvert

- *Toads and Tesselations* by Sharon Morrisette

History:

Books:

- *Heroes of History* book series

- *Horrible Histories* book series (some toilet humor here, probably best for older kids)

- The *You Wouldn't Want to Be...* book series by various authors

- *Time for Kids* history biographies by Editors of Time for Kids

- The *American Girls Collection* of books (these are chapter books, not those dolls you're thinking of!)

- *Little House on the Prairie* book series by Laura Ingalls Wilder

DVD/Videos:

- *America: The Story of Us* (DVD) (Beautifully produced video series that chronicles the key events of American History, although they have seemingly random people giving their comments on the historical events. Recommended with cautions due to intense battle scenes and some difficult topics. I watch the episode with the kids so as to explain any controversial or difficult topics. Great to introduce or to review a segment of history.)

- *American Experience* video series by PBS

- *Drive Through History* DVD series

Websites/Blogs:

- *Animated Heroes* activity books and videos (Free online printable worksheets about famous historical figures; videos of some are available on YouTube.)

Grammar:

Books:

- *Punctuation Takes A Vacation; Silent Letters Loud and Clear* and *Nouns and Verbs Have A Field Day* by Robin Pulver and Lynn Rowe Reed

- *The Girl's Like Spaghetti: Why, You Can't Manage Without Apostrophes!; Twenty Odd Ducks: Why, Every Punctuation Mark Counts!* and *Eats, Shoots and Leaves: Why Commas Really Do Make A Difference!* by Lynne Truss and Bonnie Timmons

Science:

Books:

- *The Cat in the Hat's Learning Library* series

- *First Big Book of Why* and *First Big Book of Animals* and others by National Geographic Little Kids First Big Books (various authors)

- *Handbook of Nature Study* by Anna Botsford Comstock

- *1001 Inventions That Changed the World* by Jack Challoner

- *The Big Book of What?; The Big Book of How?* and *The Big Book of Why?* by Editors of Time for Kids Magazine

- The *Getting to Know the World's Greatest Inventors and Scientists* series by Mike Venezia. (My kids love these books because they make us laugh! There's also a book series about "Composers," and "Artists").

DVD/Video/Audio:

- *Modern Marvels* video series

- *Jonathan Park* (Creation-based audio drama series) by Vision Forum

- *God of Wonders* DVD

- *Creatures That Defy Evolution* DVD series

- *The Privileged Planet* DVD (Guillermo Gonzales wrote a book with the same title; excellent documentary on the uniqueness of our planet in the solar system)

Websites/Blogs/Apps:

- The Kid Should See This (thekidshouldseethis.com)

- Built By Kids (builtbykids.com)

Bible/Character Training:

Books:

- "Character First" (characterfirst.com) character education posters, videos and pamphlets

- *The Power for True Success: How to Build Character In Your Life* by the Institute in Basic Life Principles

- *The Jesus Storybook Bible: Every Story Whispers His Name* (book and audio CD) by Sally Lloyd-Jones and Jago

- *Just Mom and Me Having Tea* by Mary J. Murray

- *Leading Little Ones to God: A Child's Book of Bible Teachings* by Marian M. Schoolland

- *The One Year Bible for Children: Daily Bible Readings for A Growing Faith*, edited by V. Gilbert Beers

Audio Dramas:

- *Chronicles of Narnia: Never Has the Magic Been So Real* and others by Focus on the Family Radio Theatre

- *The Basket of Flowers; Sir Malcolm and the Missing Prince* and others by Lamplighter Theater

Church History:

Books:

- *Christian Heroes: Then and Now* series by Janet Benge and Geoff Benge

- *Hero Tales: A Family Treasury of True Stories from the Lives of Christian Heroes* by Dave and Neta Jackson

- *Missionary Stories with the Millers* by Mildred A. Martin

- The *Lightkeeper Series* (*Ten Boys Who Changed the World* and *Ten Girls Who Changed the World*) by Irene Howat

- *Peril and Peace: Chronicles of the Ancient Church; Monks and Mystics: Chronicles of the Medieval Church* and others in the *History Lives* series by Brandon and Mindy Withrow

Additional Helpful Resources

This is not meant to be comprehensive list, but a highlight of some homeschooling resources that I've found helpful. I am not affiliated with any of these products or sites (except for my own blog), and I was not paid in any way to mention these. This is simply my list of go-to resources that I thought you might find helpful.

Free Ideas, Activities And Printables:

- Clickschooling (clickschooling.com)

- Mr. Printables (mrprintables.com)

- Free Homeschool Deals (freehomeschooldeals.com)

- Homeschool Giveaways and Freebies (homeschoolgiveaways.com)

- Confessions of A Homeschooler (confessionsofahomeschooler.com)

- Homeschool Creations (homeschoolcreations.net)

- 1 + 1 + 1= 1 (1plus1plus1equals1.com) (the ".com" offers printables; the ".net" version is the daily blog).

- Frugal Fun 4 Boys (frugalfun4boys.com)

- No Time for Flashcards (notimeforflashcards.com)

- Kids Activities Blog (kidsactivitiesblog.com)

- Spoonful (spoonful.com)

- Family Education (specifically the "School & Learning" and "Entertainment & Activities" tabs) (school.familyeducation.com)

- Living Montessori Now (livingmontessorinow.com)

- The Crafty Classroom (thecraftyclassroom.com)

- Kaboose (specifically the "Crafts" and "Games" tabs) (kaboose.com)

- Kid Activities (kidactivities.net)

- Education (education.com)

- My Pinterest Board (I have several just on homeschooling) (http://pinterest.com/TheVintageCreat/boards/)

Blogs (Homeschooling Encouragement and Advice):

- Simple Homeschool (simplehomeschool.net)

- Simply Charlotte Mason (simplycharlottemason.com)

- Fun In My Back Yard (FIMBY) (Fimby.tougas.net)

168

- Cultivated Lives (heatherhaupt.com)

- Blog, She Wrote (blogshewrote.org)

- Sacred Mundane (karipatterson.com)

- Homeschool Enrichment (homeschoolenrichment.com)

- Melissa Camera Wilkins (melissacamerawilkins.com)

- Preschoolers And Peace (preschoolersandpeace.com)

- So You Call Yourself A Homeschooler (soyoucallyourselfahomeschooler.com)

- Abundant Life: Faith, Family, Homeschool (mariannesunderland.com)

- Live Life With Your Kids (livelifewithyourkids.com)

- The Vintage Creative (thevintagecreative.com) (my site)

Relevant Posts On TheVintageCreative.com:

- "Battling Giants and Building Character" (http://wp.me/p3l0KU-9U)

- "Raising A World Changer" (http://wp.me/p3l0KU-aj)

- "Teach Them Like They Were Toddlers" (http://wp.me/p3l0KU-9E)

- "Flappers and A Five Year Old" (http://wp.me/p3l0KU-m)

- "Real Life Homeschooling: Rolling With the Punches" (http://wp.me/p3l0KU-7x)

- "Surprised By Tomatoes" (http://wp.me/p3l0KU-2z)

- "This Magic Moment" (http://wp.me/p3l0KU-B)

- "He's Calling Me" (http://wp.me/p3l0KU-a9)

- "What Your Kids Learn When You're Not Looking" (http://wp.me/p3l0KU-ae)

- "Relationships Can't Be Scheduled" (http://wp.me/p3l0KU-ac)

Books/Websites To Help With Curriculum And Planning:

- *Books Children Love: A Guide to the Best Children's Literature* by Elizabeth Laraway Wilson

- *Read for the Heart* by Sarah Clarkson

- *101 Top Picks for Homeschool Curriculum* by Cathy Duffy

- *The Homeschooler's Book of Lists: More than 250 Lists, Charts, and Facts to Make Planning Easier and Faster* by Sonya Haskins

- *The Ultimate Book of Homeschooling Ideas: 500+ Fun and Creative Learning Activities for Kids Ages 3-12* by Linda Dobson

- *Well Planned Day Family Homeschool Planner* by Rebecca Keliher

- My Well Planned Day (mywellplannedday.com — online record keeping system)

- Homeschool Tracker (homeschooltracker.com — another online record keeping system)

- Apps for Homeschooling (appsforhomeschooling.com)

- Donna Young Printables and Resources (donnayoung.org)

General Homeschooling Books:

- *Educating the Whole-Hearted Child* by Clay Clarkson with Sally Clarkson

- *For the Children's Sake: Foundations of Education for Home and School* by Susan Schaeffer Macaulay

- *The Well-Trained Mind: A Guide to Classical Education at Home* by Susan Wise Baeur

- *When Children Love to Learn: A Practical Application of Charlotte Mason's Philosophy for Today* by Elaine Cooper

- *The Unschooling Handbook: How to Use The Whole World as Your Child's Classroom* by Mary Griffith

- *Project-Based Homeschooling: Mentoring Self-Directed Learners* by Lori Pickert

- *7 Tools for Cultivating Your Child's Potential* by Zan Tyler (not specifically about homeschooling, but great for helping guide kids toward their goals)

- *Homeschooling Your Struggling Learner* by Kathy Kuhl

Homemaking Resources:

- Plantoeat.com (meal planning site that I use regularly)

- Money Saving Mom (www.moneysavingmom.com)

- *Fix, Freeze, Feast: The Delicious, Money-Saving Way to Feed Your Family* by Kati Neville and Lindsay Tkacsik

- *Large Family Logistics: The Art and Science of Managing the Large Family* by Kim Brenneman